D1405535

OPTICAL ILLUSIONS

A fiendish selection of visual twisters

350 PUZZLES

Bath · New York · Singapore · Hong Kong · Cologne · Delhi
Melbourne · Amsterdam · Johannesburg · Shenzhen

This edition published by Parragon in 2013

Parragon
Chartist House
15-17 Trim Street
Bath BA1 1HA, UK
www.parragon.com

Design and layout by Talking Design
Cover design by Talking Design
Text: Robert K. Ausbourne

See page 384 for photograph copyright details

© Parragon Books Ltd 2011

All rights reserved. No part of this publication may be reproduced, stored in a retrieval system or transmitted, in any form or by any means, electronic, mechanical, photocopying, recording or otherwise, without the prior permission of the copyright holder.

ISBN 978-1-4723-2351-4

Printed in China

contents

Optical illusions, besides being more fun than a barrel of monkeys, are for the most part research tools. Who says science can't be fun? Researchers have been using optical illusions to poke and prod at the inner workings of human perception for hundreds of years. By studying optical illusions we can learn more about how and why we see the way we do.

The ability to create and look at optical illusions is uniquely human. Why we love them, is a mystery; that we do, and treasure sharing them, is a given. Popular culture has embraced optical illusions for as long as they have existed – certainly since the Greeks built the first fluted columns. For every optical illusion science can discover or invent, an artisan will happily contribute countless variations.

The term *optical illusion* has been broadened considerably. Rainbows and mermaids are optical illusions; and so is that funny face hidden in your wallpaper pattern. Anything remotely ambiguous or quirky can be an illusion. Much of art that looks three-dimensional but is really flat is an illusion. A flat picture of a three-dimensional optical illusion is an *illusion within an illusion*. A line of telephone poles receding into the distance is an illusion; the poles don't really get smaller – it's a distortion illusion caused by distance in three-dimensions. To live in three-dimensional space is to be constantly bombarded by common everyday optical illusions.

With so many optical illusions to choose from, it is often difficult to pick out the really good ones. Not to worry! We've done the work for you. In this book you'll have access to a massive collection of the most popular optical illusions and puzzles ever to enjoy and share. There is nothing common about these illusions. You will experience the thrill of figure/ground confusion, unstable constancy, persistence of vision and a few binocular occlusions. Don't be surprised if you find yourself walking up to a complete stranger saying, 'Hey, look at this!'

001 bull run

This old Bovril advertising piece seems to show a distortion of size as we compare one bull to the other. Both bulls are the same size. The drawing's perspective is the driving force.

chapter 1

visual distortions

Have you ever heard the old saw, 'I've got a million things on my mind'? Well, it's true for all of us. We each have a million descriptions in our heads. They help us identify things, such as this is a duck, this is a tree, that's a white rock, or a black swan, or a blue monkey – the list goes on and on.

The list gets even larger when you consider the scope of descriptions we can master, such as 'Buffalo Bill's defunct who used to ride a watersmooth-silver stallion and break onetwothreefour pigeonsjustlikethat.'[1] We are maestros of the miniscule. Did you know that we have a type of neuron in our brains that does nothing but help us decide where a straight line starts and stops? It's true. No other animal can match our penchant for form and texture.

Distortion illusions cavort in our robust ability to identify texture and shape. So precise is our competency that a tiny nudge is all it takes to make us momentarily 'see' a line as bent when it is actually straight. In this chapter you will see many of the best distortion illusions ever devised, with dozens of squashed squares, distorted circles, size anomalies, bent lines and wandering centre points.

[1] Buffalo Bill's Defunct, e .e. cummings

The Banded Arrowhead is a subtle form of the Fraser Spiral (see page 31). Reversed sets of arrowheads coerce an apparent unevenness to the horizontal rows.

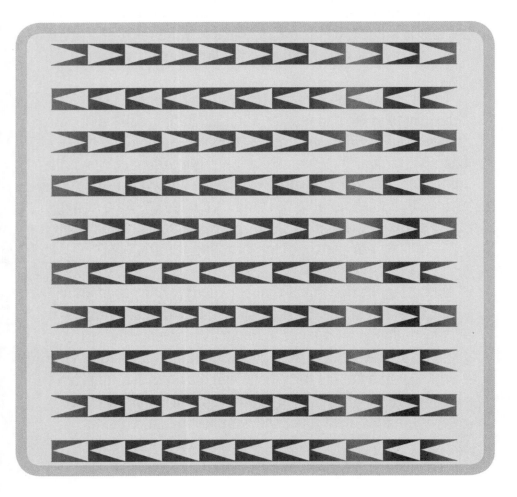

The Curved Cards is one of the oldest and best loved distortions. Except for colour the two cards are identical. Whichever card happens to be on the left always appears larger. Knowing that we will compare the long gentle curve of one card to the short choppy curve of the other ensures the illusion. Cut these shapes out and place them back to back – the illusion will disappear. Use three or even four cards placed as shown. The illusion persists.

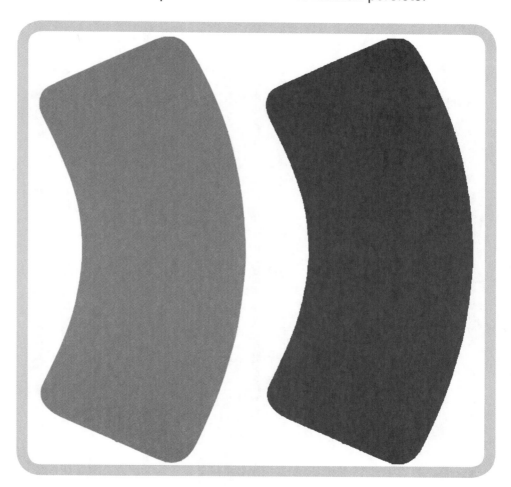

The Herring, or sometimes Wundt, distortion is named after researchers who studied its effects more than 100 years ago. The background patterns cause the effect and the bars in the foreground are targets for distortion. The bars can seem to bend inwards or outwards at a whim of the background.

The Herring, or sometimes Wundt, distortion is named after researchers who studied its effects more than 100 years ago. The background patterns cause the effect and the bars in the foreground are targets for distortion. The bars can seem to bend inwards or outwards at a whim of the background.

In this Herring variation the bars appear to bend inwards
and outwards in the same illusion.

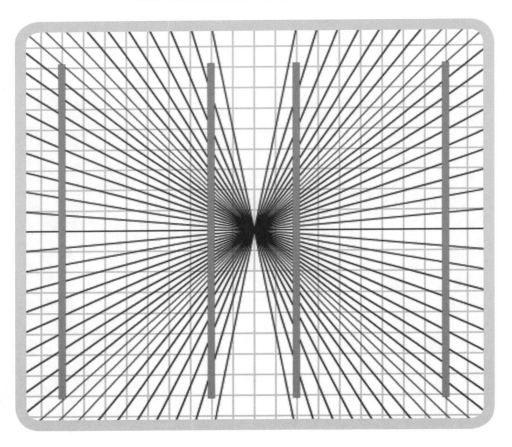

In this Herring variation the background is in the front and our view of the circle is subject to distortion.

008 café wall

The Café Wall distortion was discovered on an tiled storefront
in Bristol. Even though they are uniform, these rows of tiles appear
bent and uneven. The amount of offset in the black
and white tiles, and the thickness of the grout lines are
influential in this distortion.

The Hidden Chain distortion happens when we try to track an oblique line behind an obstruction. The two parts of the continuous chain that we can see do not appear to meet behind the board, but they do.

chequerboard bulge

Chequerboard distortions are a rich source of illusory effects. The chequerboard design underneath is uniform and perfect. The distorted appearance is caused by objects placed in the foreground. A ruler will verify that all vertical and horizontal lines are actually straight.

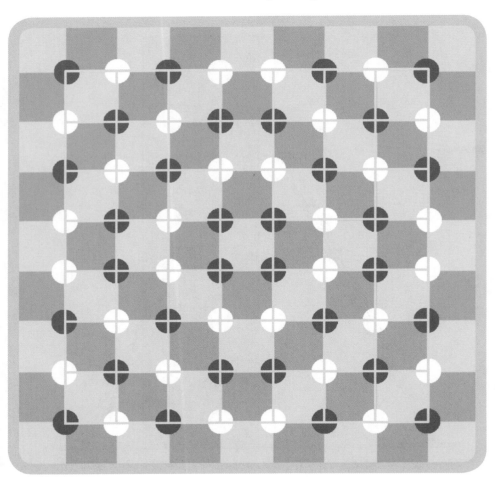

In this Chequerboard variation the distortion is generated by a simple pattern of tiny stars.

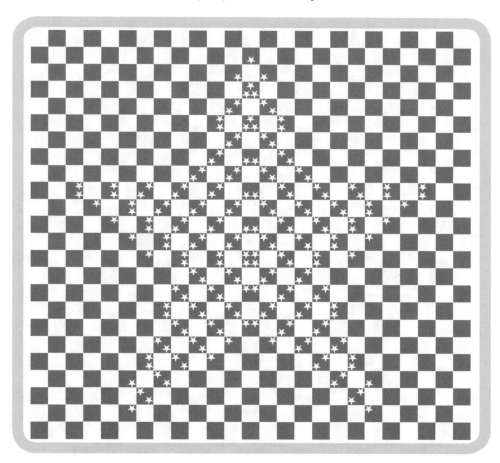

In this Chequerboard variation a wavy distortion is achieved by applying a pattern of tiny squares.

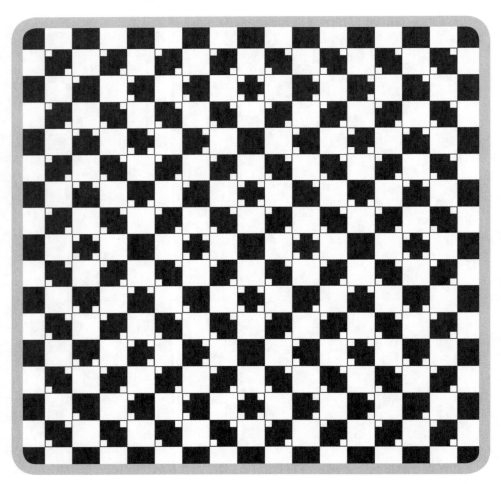

An extravagant formula of shapes gives this Chequerboard variation a three-dimensional rippling appearance.

Tiny gears replace the circles in this Chequerboard variation.

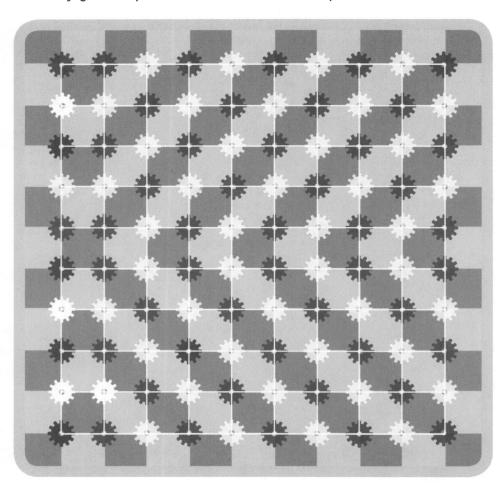

This is a Herring distortion mutation in which a circle is bent by a chevron-shaped background.

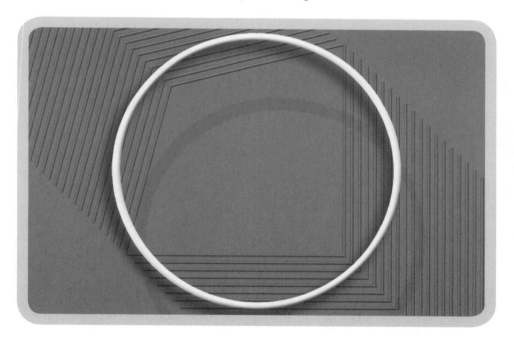

The circles in the background deceive us and cause the square in the centre to appear bent when it is really straight. It may be that the concentric circles fool our brains into thinking that we must be moving. The square looks distorted and foreshortened as it might appear if we were moving.

In this Herring variation the circles in the background cause the square in the foreground to appear to bow inwards. The sparks are just for show.

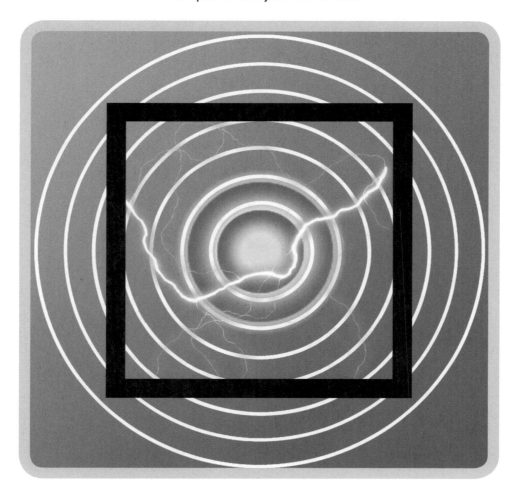

All of the vertical lines and dashes shown in this variation of the Fraser Spiral (see page 31) are straight up and down.

The Crooked Gate distortion looks lopsided by using the same effects as the Fraser Spiral (see page 31).

delboeuf illusion

Which black circle is bigger in the Delboeuf Illusion? They are the same size. Both objects are influenced by their nearest neighbours, and we are presented with another distortion illusion.

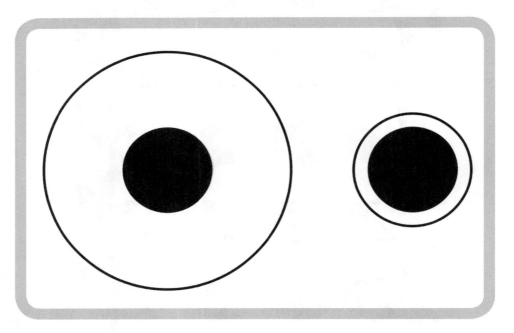

This is a three-dimensional version of the classic Titchener Illusion. Which of the central balls is larger? Both are the same size.

022 Fraser illusion rope

This variation of the Fraser Spiral, or Braided Rope effect (see opposite page), makes these horizontal rows of diamond shapes appear crooked.

Here is the classic Fraser Spiral distortion illusion. The Spiral is not really a spiral. It is actually a series of concentric circles. The twisted ropelike, 'braided' design of the circles makes us think we see a spiralling pattern.

The 'stop sign' shape is being distorted by arrowheads, which have been placed slightly off-kilter in this distortion illusion.

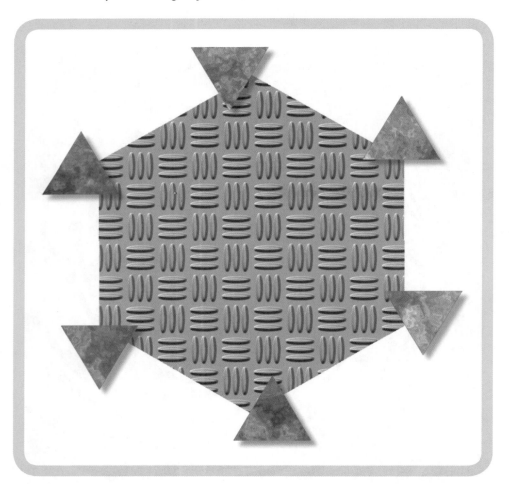

How high is the ball on the face of the Halfway Pyramid? Is it halfway up, 60 per cent, or maybe 80 per cent? The ball is exactly halfway up the pyramid. It is a distortion caused by the slopping sides of the triangle shape. Count the 'rings' on the pyramid to prove it. The rings are evenly spaced, even though they appear closer together near the top (see Pyramid Dots, page 46).

Here is the classic Herring distortion illusion shown in reverse, where the horizontal lines appear to be bent inwards.

The Horizon illusion is one of perspective. The two images shown side by side are identical, yet they give the impression of being radically different in perspective. The distortion is caused by the fact that the images are touching and because the brain wants to assume they are a single image. If this is so, then all objects must point towards a single vanishing point on the horizon. However, they don't, and we perceive a distortion.

This example illustrates the fact that we almost always assume light comes from above. It is difficult to visualize the first, third, and fifth segments in the Shadow Stick as anything but humplike. The remaining segments appear cuplike and concave. If the shadows were reversed, we would still assume the light was coming from above and see the humps as hollows and hollows as humps.

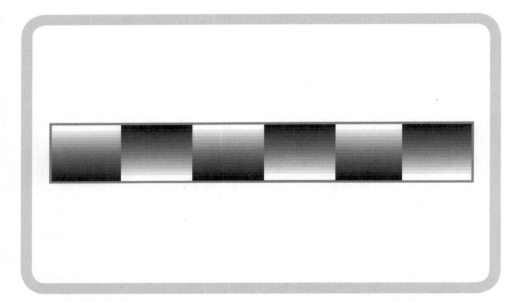

Which Leprechaun is larger? They are actually the same size in this whimsical variation of the classic Titchener illusion (see page 29).

Here is the classic Lincoln's Hat illusion. The president's stovepipe hat is exactly as high as its brim is wide. The rule: A vertical line that intersects a horizontal line will always appear longer.

In this Lincoln's Hat variation (see opposite page), the distance between dot one on the left in the horizontal row and the dot overhead is the same as the distance between dot one and dot three on the right in the horizontal row. The rule: A vertical line that intersects a horizontal line will always appear longer in comparison.

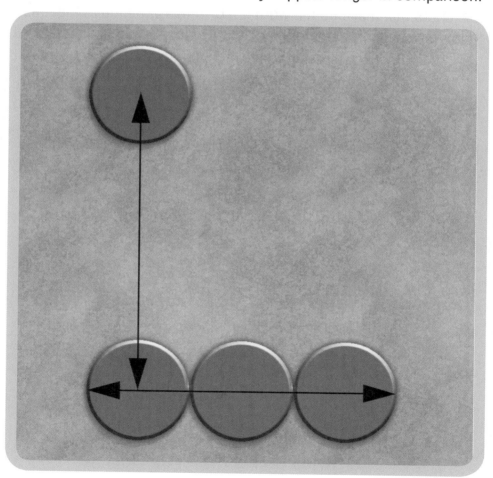

The letters that make up the word 'LIFE' in this variation of the Fraser Spiral (see page 31) are not crooked; they just look that way. Grab a ruler and prove it to yourself.

The Mystic Wheel's spokes are all flat, yet we cannot help but to perceive the wheel as three-dimensional. The ripples in the spokes become either humps or hollows. Any ripple will appear hollow on one side of the design and humped on the other. If you turn the design upside down, the humps and hollows will remain the same because we assume the light source hasn't changed.

The Obama Illusion presents two faces of the president side by side.
They both look fairly reasonable except that they are upside down.
Turn the image right side up and get a big surprise! We are very
good at recognizing faces, but recognizing individual facial features
is a whole other kettle of fish.

Which ball looks the biggest in this scene? Both balls are the same size, and the drawing's perspective is causing the distortion.

This is the classic Poggendorf Illusion. Which of the black lines is continuous from top to bottom? A ruler will prove that it is the lowest line on the right that is connected to the top line segment. If the lines were all horizontal or vertical, we would have no trouble tracking them behind the obstruction. However, oblique lines give us a little distortional trouble.

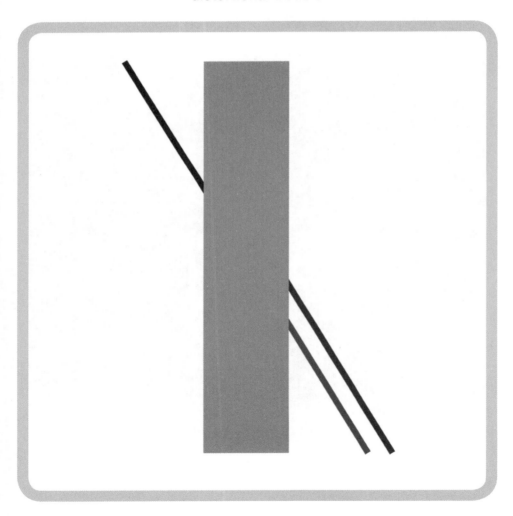

A classic distortion called the Ponzo Illusion after a researcher: this distortion is caused by an 'assumed' perspective. We assume that the peaked line segment must act similar to a railroad track; it should get smaller in the distance. The horizontal lines are the same length, but the top one appears longer because we assume it must be farther away on the tracks.

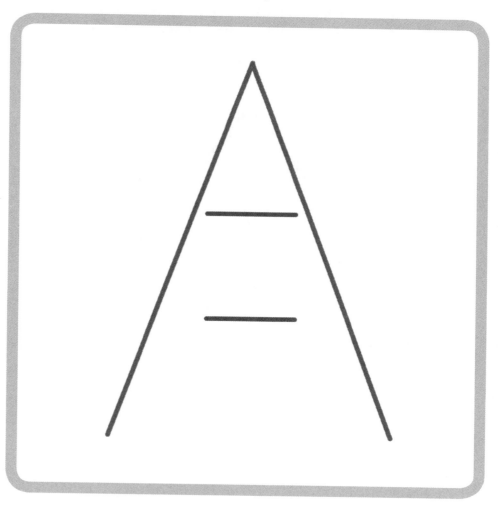

Here is a plan view of the classic Pyramid distortion illusion.
Which of the vertical dots most closely marks the centre of the
triangle? If you think it is number three, guess again.
Dot number two most closely marks the centre.

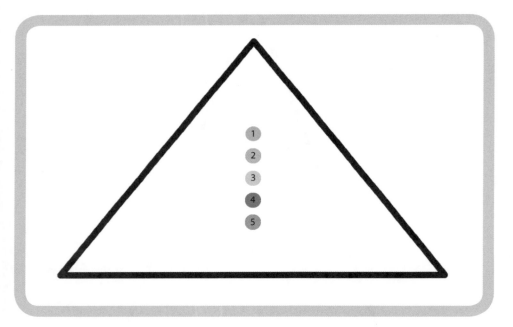

This illusion illustrates the power and treachery of images. There is no real perspective here; it's just ink on a page. Each dot merely gets skinnier as they progress across the image. Yet our brains are happy to assume that there is real depth and a gentle curve.

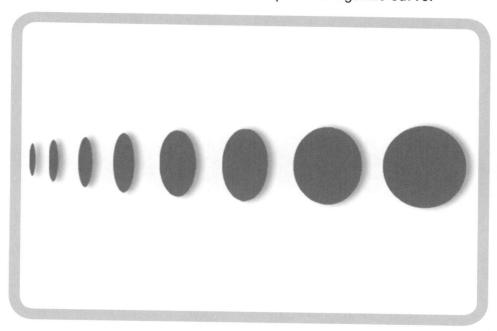

In this design of a mirrored sine wave the vertical dashes are all identical. They only appear to be shorter or longer according to their position within the wave.

In this variation of the Horizon distortion illusion (see page 35), we are presented with two views of a building. The images are identical, yet one building looks like it is leaning at a different angle. We are assuming that the two images are one, and, therefore, both buildings should point at the same place in the sky.

In the classic Zöllner, or sometimes Herringbone Illusion, reversed herringbone patterns on the parallel lines distort our perception and to us the lines look crooked.

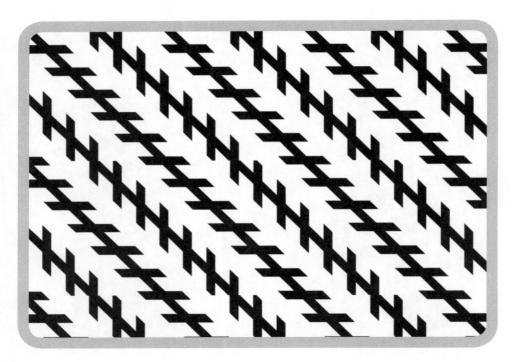

This variation of the Zöllner Illusion (see opposite page) uses reversed segments of chains to accomplish the distortion of the horizontal symmetry.

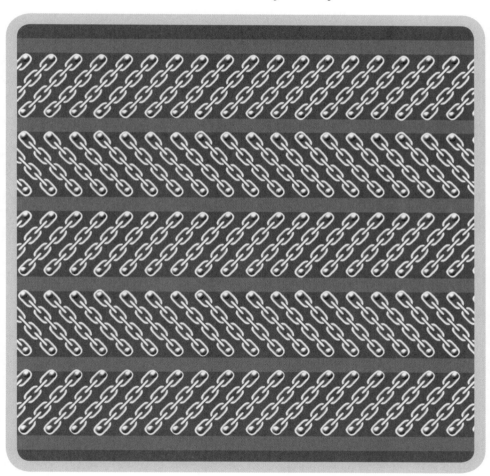

The Palm Tree distortion is a variation of the Zöllner Illusion (see page 50). Here, a herringbone pattern of lines makes the trees appear to lean in different directions.

This variation of the Zöllner Illusion (see page 50) is self-explanatory.

ARE THE LINES IN THIS PARAGRAPH PARALLEL?

THEY MAY OR MAY NOT BE. BUT DON'T BET THE

HOUSE UNTIL YOU MEASURE THE ANGLE. IT IS

A SPACIAL DISTORTION ILLUSION BASED ON

A SUBTLE MISDIRECTION OF PERSPECTIVE.

046 all is vanity

The All is Vanity print is perhaps the most popular ambiguous illusion of all time. Millions of copies have been sold since the print was first introduced in 1902. It has an allegorical theme inspired by a biblical quote from King Solomon, 'Vanity of vanities, all is vanity.' We are left on our own to guess the allegory message, but its ambiguity is clear. It is either a pretty girl admiring herself in a vanity mirror, or a huge skull lurking in the background.

Charles Allen Gilbert, *All is Vanity*, 1892

chapter 2

ambiguous figures

Ambiguous figures can be *taken* in more than one way. Each way that a figure can be taken is complete in itself. It has its own story, its own contours, the works. Each way an image can be taken is also called an *aspect* of the image, and having taken an aspect, one has obtained closure.

One curious thing about ambiguous figures is that many viewers can see both aspects at the same time. This is easy to believe because once we obtain closure, we often find it much easier to flip back and forth between aspects willy-nilly.

'Not!' Say the scientists. The speed of vision is not like the speed of light; it isn't that fast. There is a built-in, one-tenth-of-a-second delay between the time we perceive a thing, and the time when we 'see' the thing in our mind. Call it processing time. It may not sound like much, but at the quantum level at least, it is impossible to perceive multiple aspects at exactly the same time.

In this chapter you will find boundless ambiguity, from the simple to the sublime. Obtain closure with fanciful drawings and three-dimensional constructs. Battle figure/ground confusion and stave off perceptual instability. Find out whether you are inside or outside, on the top or on the bottom? Remember to always look for the 'other thing' and have fun.

Two aspects share the same contours in this figure;
one wine glass and two bottles.

What do you see here? In this elegant ambiguity there are
two glasses and one bottle – with cork.

The Missing Corner Illusion has three aspects: 1) a cube with a missing corner in the front; 2) a hollow room with two walls and a floor, with a small cube sitting in the back corner; and 3) a large cube with a small cube floating separately in front. Note: Build a model of this illusion – rotate the model in your hand and watch as the little cube in aspect (3) rotates backwards!

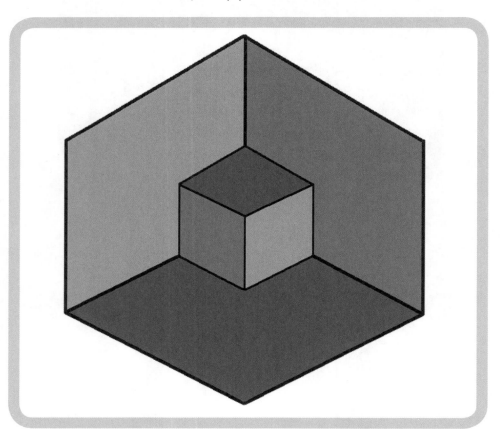

This patterned rendering of the Missing Corner Illusion (see opposite page) may help us obtain closure with all three aspects.

Illustration by Arthur Azevedo

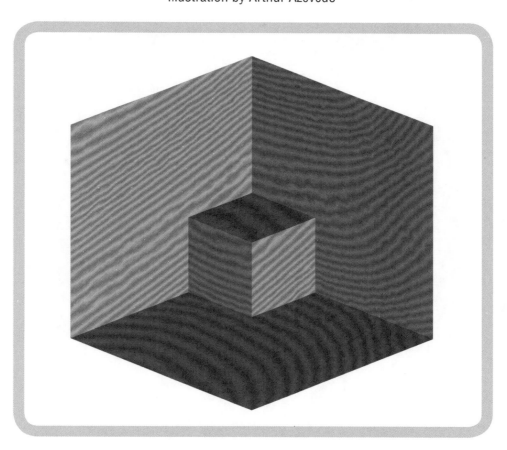

This old Japanese print is called the Ten Cats illusion.
Can you find all ten cats?

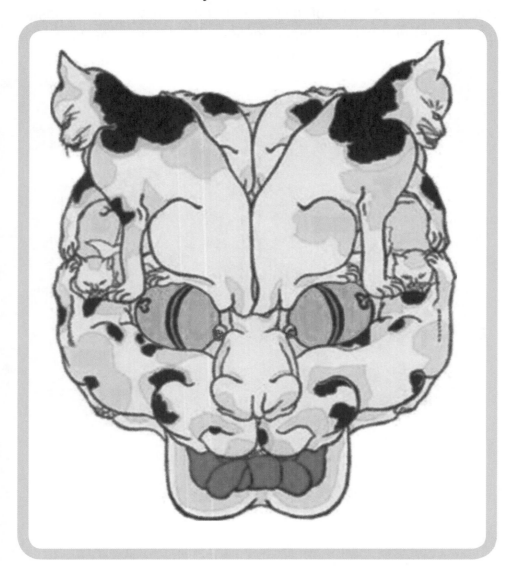

This illustration from *Alice's Adventures in Wonderland* contains an ambiguous illusion. Can you find it? The caterpillar's legs are serving duel purposes. On the lower half of the caterpillar the legs are just legs; but on the head they serve as the caterpillar's face in profile. Ambiguity is where you find it.

Illustrated by John Tenniel, from *Alice's Adventures in Wonderland*, 1862

This three-dimensional figure can be seen as three blocks with a cross-shaped piece missing from the front, or the cross shape can be seen as floating in front of the blocks.

The Reversible Stairs is another classic. In this view the steps have grey tops and a black background. Flip the image over and the steps now have grey fronts and a white background.

055 ambiguous pillars

In *Piliers de l'ambiguïté,* or the Ambiguous Pillars, there is something about these columns that makes them ambiguous. If you look closely at the spaces between the columns, you will find several figures in profile.

The Candle and Lovers Illusion is a crafty ambiguity.
Can you avoid figure/ground confusion and find both the lovers and
the candle? Hint: The candle is in the foreground, and the lovers are
part of the background.

This drawing shows a young couple daydreaming beside a lake. Can you find what they are dreaming about? A baby maybe?

Several scientists were studying this photo of a distant planet. They were arguing about what it could be. Some were sure it was a natural feature, while others leaned towards a lava bulge getting ready to erupt. They argued for hours until a worker walked by and innocently turned the picture around. Turn the picture around yourself and see what the humbled scientists saw.

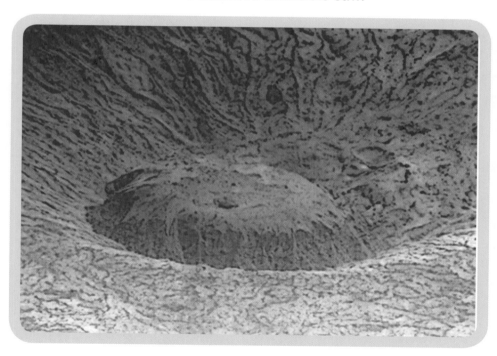

The Book Illusion can be seen as open and facing you; or open and facing away from you. Can you obtain closure with both aspects?

This old poster from Buffalo Bill's Wild West Show is a drawing of Buffalo Bill made entirely of related objects. How many can you find?

cats in a pattern

This tessellated pattern has grey cats facing to the right.
Can you find the black cats? Hint: Flip the image over.

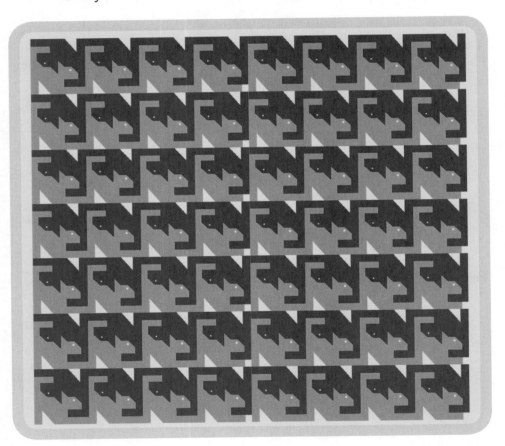

Do you see a tunnel in this geometric pattern?
Do you see a cone shape?

In this Field of Cubes, do you see the cubes with dark bases? Or with dark tops? A canny viewer in complete closure will see both.

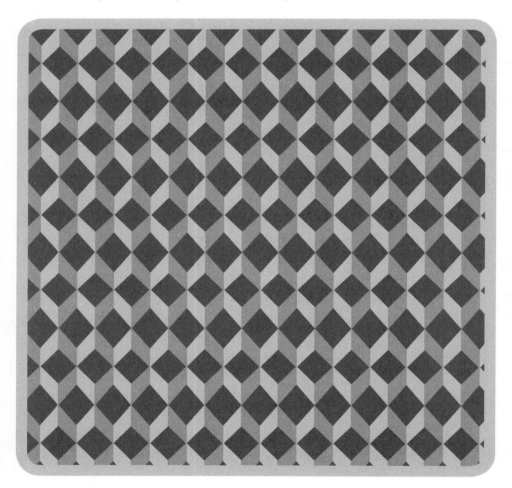

Do you see dimples in the centre and bumps all around in the Bumpy Plate Illusion? Can you imagine that the light comes from below and see bumps in the centre and dimples all around?

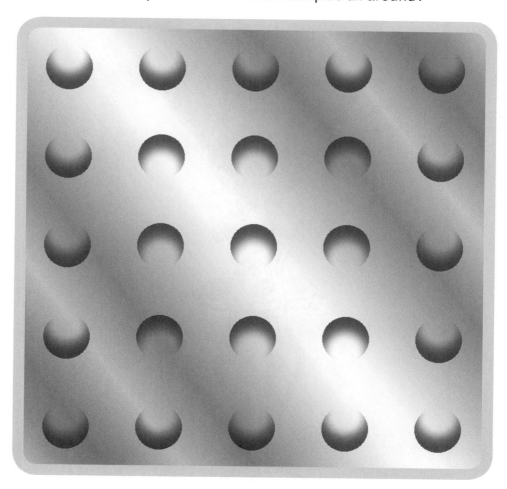

This objet d'art from an illustrated catalogue comes complete with two open-mouthed profiles. Can you find them?

The Telephone Illusion is so old that this instrument wouldn't work for texting. But then again, my smart phone doesn't have profiles of two cute dogs built into the design.

The Eight Illusion shows the figure 8 cutout of wood sitting in a large circle, which is also cut out of wood. Rotate the image 180 degrees. The background is now solid wood, and the figure 8 is part of the background!

Illustration by Arthur Azevedo

Can you find a Native American Chief and an Eskimo in this drawing?

This illusion is either a toothy, bearded guy with dark glasses, or a strongman lifting a barbell.

Do you see the falcon bird design in this illusion,
or the face of Professor Falcon?

This illusion is simply ambiguous. Do you see a whiskered mouse, or a smiling man?

Is this a slipper, or a man with dark hair and glasses?

In the Father and Son illusion, can you find them both?
Hint: the old man's prominent nose has a bump, which is very close
to the son's Roman nose.

The Third Generation Illusion contains a portrayal of the daughter, the mother, and the grandfather. Can you find all three? Hint: The mother needs the daughters choker, the grandfather does not. Good luck!

This charming painting of two tropical fish kissing is hiding
an owl in plain sight. Can you find the hooter?
Hint: The owl takes an eye from each.

The Necker Cube is a famous wire-framed rectangle that can change spatial geometry in a twinkle as you watch. The small end in front can face forwards or backwards, but the top is always the top. The fish looks like it is inside, and then sometimes outside the 'tank.'

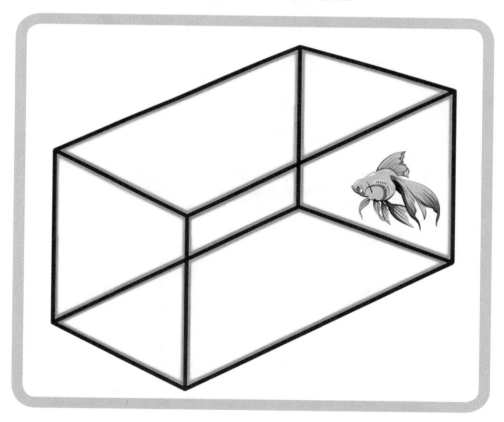

This pen and ink drawing can be seen as either a woman wrapped in a blanket, or the clenched fist of someone that needs a manicure.

Contrasting hues and shades on the Folded Star illusion give it three-dimensional look, which causes it to appear folded in various directions.

This richly illustrated example of the multiple-face type illusion is so old that it may be one of the first of its kind. The young girl faces away in profile; the old hag faces left with a choker for a mouth. The choker (mouth) element appears omnipresent in all variations.

This Figure/Ground Illusion also has two profiles. The *figure* of the vase is in the foreground; the profiles belong, for the most part, to the *background* – hence, figure/ground illusion.

Gossip, and Satan Came Also is another popular allegorical print from the last century. We see two gossips chatting in the market while the face of a devil lurks in the background.

George Wotherspoon, circa 1900

In this illustration we see the farm, the workers, and the sheep but where is the farmer?

Answer: Rotate the images 90 degrees counterclockwise. Some trees make the farmer's face, and the moon is near his right ear.

Is this a drawing of a goose flying west, or a hawk flying east?
Okay, the direction doesn't matter.

Is this a drawing of the cutest little Mouse, and the cutest little Hippo?

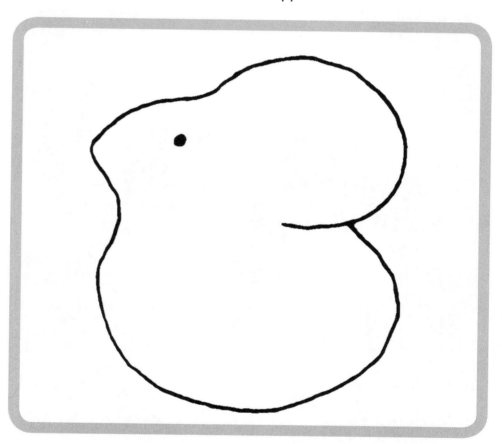

Today and Tomorrow is another allegory/skull theme from long ago. Here, we see the happy couple celebrating as a skulking skull lurks in the background.

H. M. Rose, circa 1900

The outline of Idaho has a locally famous ambiguous illusion along their state border. Can you find the old potato farmer? Of course, Montana, the next state over must have the same illusion in reverse, right? Can you find the old sheep herder?

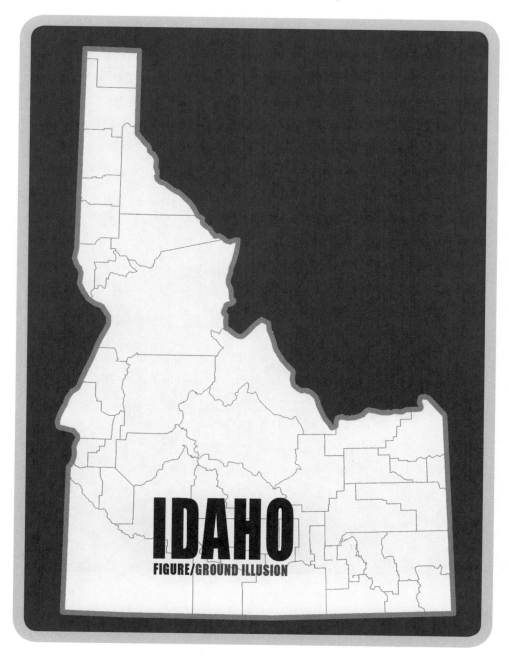

IDAHO
FIGURE/GROUND ILLUSION

This painting of Christ from around the early twentieth century has become iconic because of the eyes. If you stare at them long enough, they seem to open and close.

Gabriel Max, *Veronica's Handkerchief,* 1915

Is this a picture of whales leaping joyfully among the waves?
Turn the page 90 degrees anti-clockwise to see what it really is.

Answer: A man's face can be seen near the waterline.

This patriotic urn celebrates the sixteenth president of the United States. Find his profile and identify the man.

This design for an iron hitching post has Abraham Lincoln's face all over it – literally. The president's profile, with beard and famous hat, are wrapped continuously around the post. It, doesn't matter how you view it, there are always two profiles to see.

This a drawing of a Lion leaping from the undergrowth, or a flower.
Our minds are happy to recognize either.

At first we see a man, but a closer look reveals a pretty girl with a baby. Can you see both?

A lurking skull is featured in yet another allegorical print. This time the skull is bound by bowers of greenery and some wine.

The Marble Winged Butterfly is one of the most beautiful denizens … wait, make those two Marble Winged Butterflies, mating.

The Mermaid Illusion shows a posing mermaid and a crone, which share the same space in this drawing.

Within the foreground colour (black) of this design there is a row of female forms, while in the background colour (white) there is a line of hooded nuns.

In this contemporary interpretation of the Old Woman–Young Girl Illusion, the action is reversed, and the young girl's choker is well-suited to an old woman.

The Penguin Illusion shows the flightless bird carrying around a profile of Abe Lincoln. Can you find it?

This old advertising card uses an ambiguous reflection of two lovers with cloak-like shadows to sell flatware. There is no spoon like an old spoon.

A Pierrot's Love. This old French postcard is another twist on the Lovers and Skull theme (see page 102). This time it is the famous clown who is tempting fate.

This antique pipe was handcrafted in Switzerland with the profile of President Roosevelt right around the bole – can you see the profile in the cast shadow? The illustration is also homage to Rene Magritte's famous painting, *Ceci n'est pas une pipe* (This is not a pipe). This is not a pipe either; it's merely a picture of a pipe.

This is not a pipe casting a shadow profile.

The front of this Pizza Box is pointing forward twice!

The Rabbit—Duck Illusion is more than 100 years old and still quacks proud. It is either a duck facing to the left, or a rabbit facing to the right.

Turn the smoking pipe around 180 degrees to see Santa Claus.

Drawing by Paul Agule

Paul Agule

The saxophone player is hiding a woman's face. Can you find her?

The elephant looks like an elephant; where is the seashell?

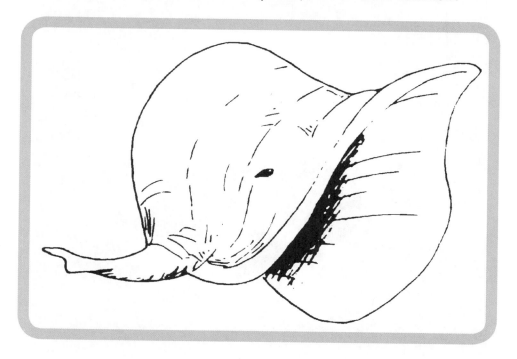

This ambiguous example is from a modern movie poster for a movie called *Shrooms*. Here, the skull theme is aided by a few well-placed mushrooms.

This old political cartoon uses the skull theme to best advantage.

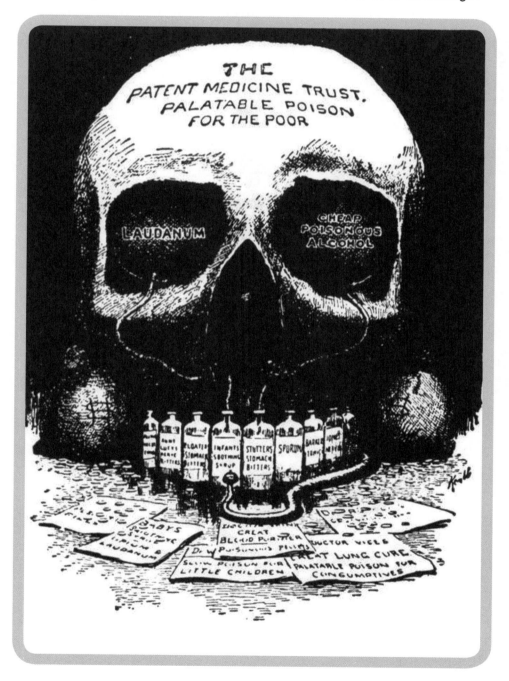

The Seven Clowns illusion is a favourite because of its multiple aspects. Can you spot all seven clowns in this figure?

This ambiguous figure is called the Sleeping Dog Illusion –
what? It looks like a picture of the Elephant Man! Can you find the
sleeping dog? Hint: Rotate the image 90 degrees clockwise.

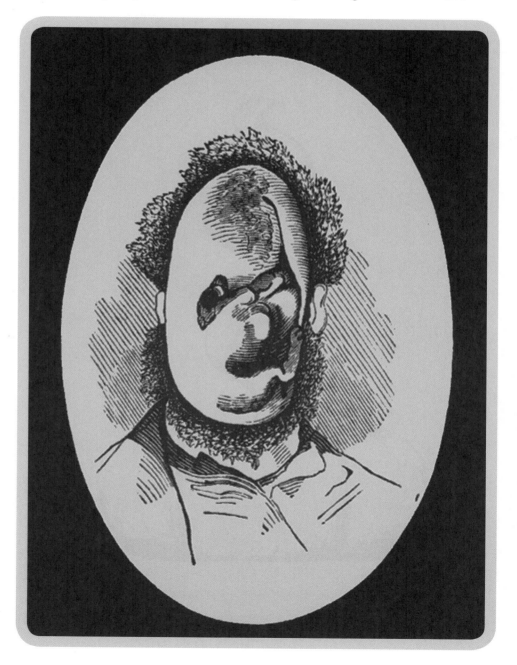

The Cork Screw Illusion is also an Indian basket with
a rearing cobra snake.

The Swan Illusion is also the Squirrel Illusion.
Can you spot both aspects?

This design can have four blocks with stars on the tops, or three blocks with stars on the bases.

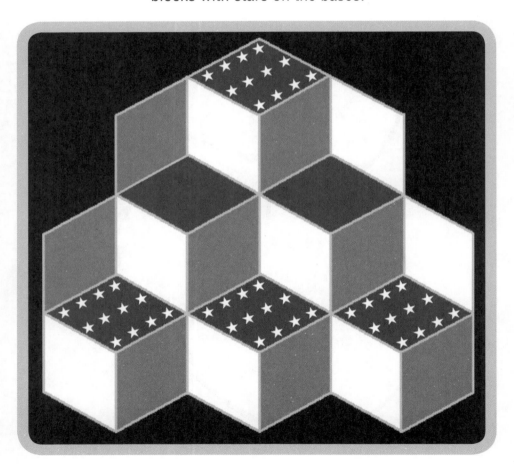

You might see six blocks with stars on top, or six blocks with stars on the bases.

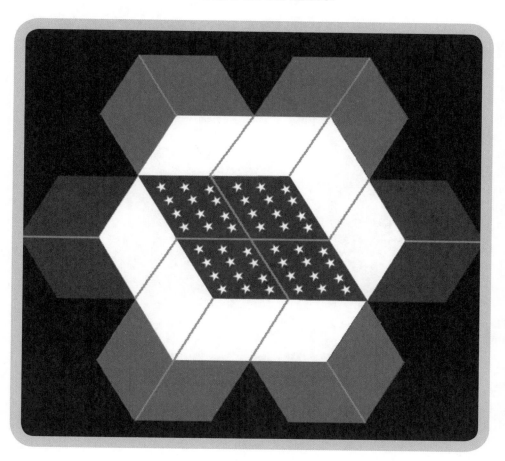

This is our second example from the pen of George Wotherspoon, called *Society: a Portrait.* It shows a dandy out on the town with his girlfriends. Gosh, this fellow really looks like an Ass!

George Wotherspoon, circa 1900

On this Civil war era trading card, the card reads, 'The Eagle of the Republic: what do you see in this picture?'

L. Prang & Co., Country Clerks Office of the District Court of Mass., 1865

Answer: The design contains the hidden faces of Jefferson Davis, George Washington, and Abraham Lincoln.

With a written form as robust as the English language, there is bound to be ambiguities. In this figure the letter 'A' could easily stand for the letter 'H.'

THE CAT

An old postcard illustration called, *The Tie That Binds* blends a woman's figure with a necktie to create ambiguity.

The Three or Four Blocks Illusion is the classic three-dimensional cube illusion. Do you see three square blocks or four? Hint: The fourth block is an ambiguous construction in the centre.

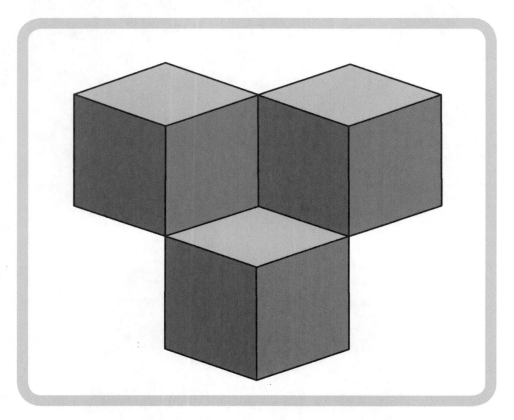

This figure is called the Tao Mouse Illusion. The Tao symbol is the sole of ambiguity, yin–yang, good–evil, black–white. If you see a mouse here too, you are well on the path to contentment and closure.

This is a drawing by the 18th-century English artist William Hogarth, called *Time Smoking a Picture – While Statues Molder into Worth*. The inscription reads: '*For nature and your self-appeal, ner learn of others what to feel.*'

The Time Passes illusion shows an older woman who's face is made up of images from her own life.

How many tools can you identify in the Tool Set Illusion? Don't forget figure/ground confusion, and count tools in the background as well!

Answer: There are many tools pictured here, both in the foreground and background. Find as many as you can.

Oh no! Not another Turkey—Eskimo Illusion!

This whimsical old sketch is both an island and a
reclining bearded man.

Wenzel Hollar, circa fifteenth century

The earliest known version of the Young–Old Woman Illusion
and probably the original, this delightfully ambiguous figure is called,
My Wife and My Mother-in-Law.

Illustrated by W. E. Hill, from *Puck* magazine, 1915

Cartoonists are wonderful sources of ambiguity. The caption of the cartoon reads; '*A curious optical illusion caused by a lady forgetting the number of her bathing machine.*'
Illustrated by William Heath Robinson

A photo taken in 1981 during a test flight of a U.S. fighter jet has an amazing ambiguity. The cast shadow below the jet makes it look like it is flying low to the ground, and yet the surrounding terrain features indicate that the fighter must be huge – way out of scale. What is going on? Hint: The cast shadow is really a large lake far below the jet.

What is the Woman of the World Illusion? Where is the ambiguity?
Hint: The title, plus what is round and has continents?

Hidden among the major continents and oceans
is the outline of a woman's head.

What do these blobs of ink mean? Hint: Think; Mercator Projection, or rotate the image?

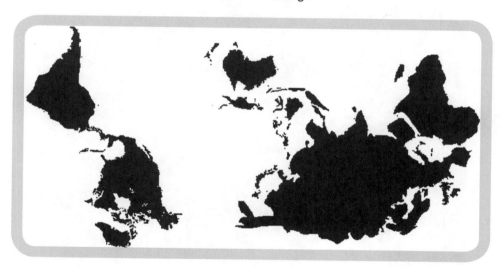

131 chieftain rock

Yosemite National Park

chapter 3

faces in nature

From the time we are born faces become important to us; our survival depends on it. We start figuring them out long before we are able to recognize our own face. An entire region of our brains is devoted to faces. Looking at faces closely, every day, throughout our lives makes us extremely good at facial recognition.

It is no surprise that we remain fascinated by faces all our lives. We not only see them on other people's heads, we see faces in clouds, in mountain crags, in wallpaper patterns, on pansies and in leafy litter. We see a face on the Moon, distant planets and even in the random patterns of the stars.

This chapter has a collection of some of our favourite faces from out-of-the-way places, plus more free-range ambiguous sightings.

The east rim of the Grand Canyon.

A face staring upwards to the sky in Bandon, Oregon.

59 rue de Rivoli, Paris, France

This Samurai Crab is shown sporting a believable mask of an ancient Japanese warrior. The story has it that this species of crab only looked a little like a Japanese warrior in the beginning. Centuries of fishermen taking the crabs, and honourably releasing those crabs that looked most like samurai, and which lived to reproduce, have fostered the contemporary picture-perfect Samurai Crab. Could this be a case of unnatural selection?

Rijksmuseum van Natuurlijke Historie, Leiden, the Netherlands

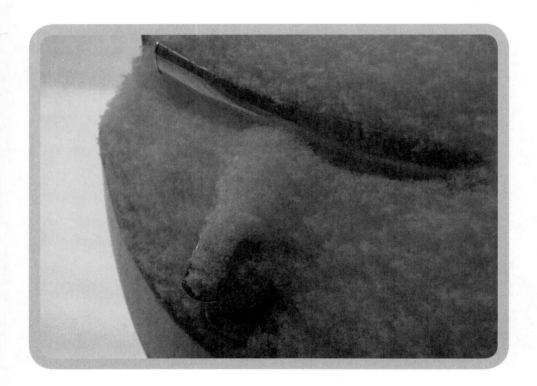

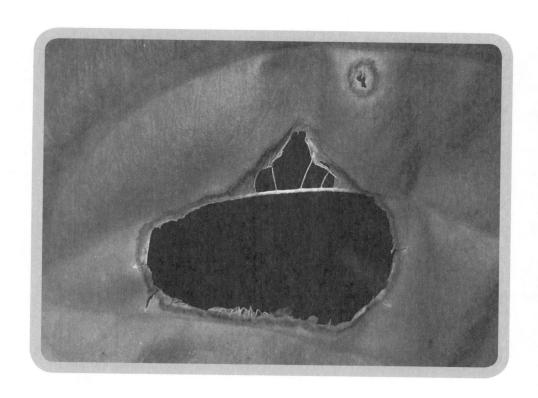

'Those are not the Droids you want'. This is a camera used for videoconferencing.

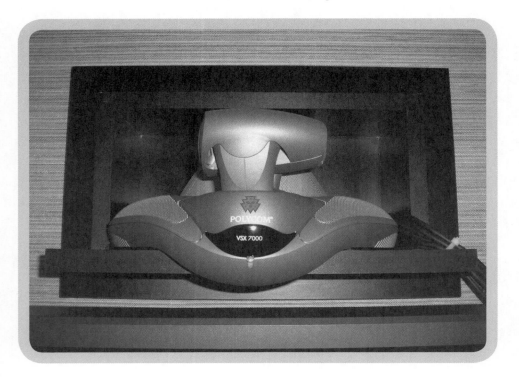

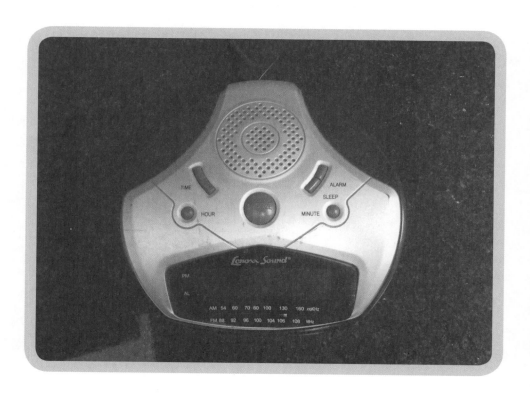

Medicine Lodge State Park.

Ship Rock in the Navaho Indian Nation, near the town of Shiprock, New Mexico.

MERRY

CHRISTMAS

150 reverse christmas

Can you help round up Jack Frost's reindeer?

chapter 4

topsy-turvies

Topsy-Turvies, or Reversible Illusions, are ambiguous because they contain separate aspects, use the same doodles and are occupying the same place. The difference is that topsy-turvy aspects are upside down; you have to rotate these images in order to see all aspects. We've placed these illusions in one spot for convenience, and to show you how to solve the puzzles.

Topsy-turvies are also anamorphic because they are changelings, depending upon how you look at them. If you don't look at an anamorphic ambiguity differently, it might not change, and you might miss seeing a new aspect. In that case it will just be a topsy.

Get ready to turn head over heels for this collection!

151 arcimboldo vegetables

Turn this image upside down to see why fans refer to
Giuseppe Arcimboldo lovingly as 'Old Fruit Face'.

Giuseppe Arcimboldo, *Man in the Fruit Bowl*

Help this street-hardened detective 'Find the Killer'.

A frog is looking for tasty flies, and hopes a nearby horse
has brought some. Can you find the horse?

Old Dobbins is waiting patiently for his owner.
Can you help find him?

An old Japanese print shows an angry fellow.
Can you cheer him up?

This old gentleman looks upon life with disappointment and regret. Can you change his disposition?

This British bulldog is from a popular series of topsy-turvies published during World War I. Reverse the image to see the German Kaiser 'on the run.'

Here, the Kaiser is looking behind with a worried look, while Lord Kitchener is winking and smiling.

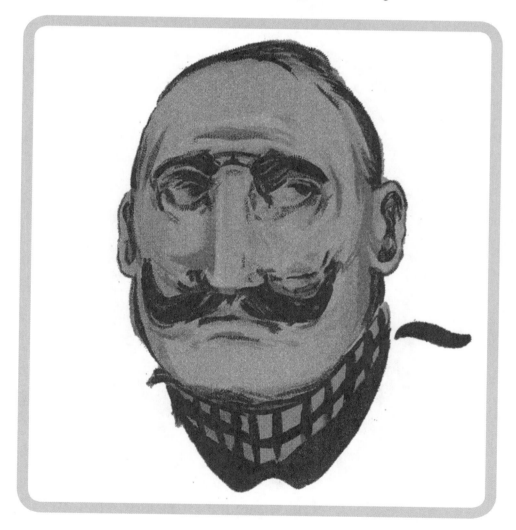

Kaiser Wilhelm II, and where is his British adversary, Lord Kitchener?

Once again the two warriors are contrasted in reverse.

A monk has come to the priory seeking help.
Can you help find his missing twin?

Cartoonist Peter Newell was very popular for his Topsy-Turvy books and cartoons. For a time, the entire nation was 'flipping' over his work.

Peter Newell, *Topsys and Turvys, Topsys and Turvys Number 2,* 1893

A hermit with a long red beard dwelt in a lonely place.

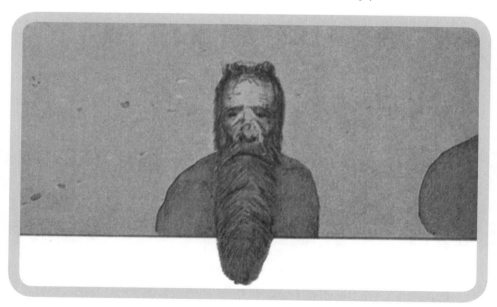

The squirrel gazed with wonder upon his gloomy face

A Peter Newell story about Fernando and his cradle…

Peter Newell, *Topsys and Turvys, Topsys and Turvys Number 2,* 1893

Fernando bears his cradle in, a cradle strong and deep.

Then, placing it upon a rug, he rocks himself to sleep.

A Peter Newell cartoon of Piggy and the Wolves.
Peter Newell, *Topsys and Turvys, Topsys and Turvys Number 2,* 1893

In hope of pork, two small grey wolves watched all one autumn day.

But Piggy smelled a rat, and went another way.

This reversible is often found with the caption,
'Before 8 beers, and after.'

Cheerful man becomes thoughtful sage.

Faces, faces. Who's got more faces?

More faces?

Faces sharing noses.

My mother-in-law's pet monkey keeps eating my flowers; she does, too. Where is she?

Don't we look silly?

This old woodcut cartoon shows both Father and Son.

The story of the Hunter and Mother Bear by Peter Newell.

Peter Newell, *Topsys and Turvys, Topsys and Turvys Number 2,* 1893

The hunter found two bear-cubs and took them from their cave.

But when the mother bear returned,
he fled his life to save.

Hunting Dogs and Hares, by Peter Newell

Peter Newell, *Topsys and Turvys, Topsys and Turvys Number 2,* 1893

Why do these scurrying, frightened hares come coursing through the vale?

*Because they know three hunting dogs
are close upon their trail.*

The Japanese Jugglers, by Peter Newell.

Peter Newell, *Topsys and Turvys, Topsys and Turvys Number 2,* 1893

The juggling Japanese come out, they bow and smile sweetly.

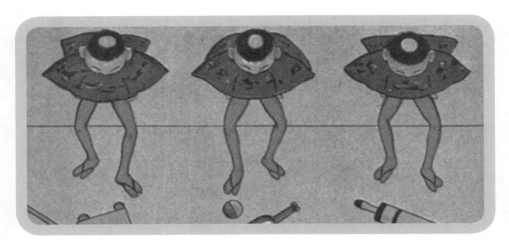

Then everything is kicked in the air,
and kept there quite a while.

Two darling Old Biddies; which would make the best grandmother?

Cartoonist Gustav Verbeek published many popular reversible cartoon stories. Every six panels held twelve panels of storyline.

12. They catch him and carry him home, where he plays with them very nicely. He becomes very fond of his master and mistress, and, if you go to call on them, you may very well see the elephant curled up on Lady Lovekins's lap.

1. Lovekins and Muffaroo see an enormous elephant rolling on his back in the grass. They manage to steal away quietly before he sees them. That is narrow escape number one.

11. "After him," cries Lovekins, "You go one way and I'll go the other."

2. Later on, Lovekins picks up a curious bottle containing some strange liquid. "Don't drink it," says Muffaroo, but Lovekins touches a drop of liquid to her tongue.

10. Then Lovekins and Muffaroo have to run to keep him in sight, for he has jumped into the grass and scurried into the woods.

3. Instantly she feels herself growing smaller, but by vigorous spitting, she saves herself from losing more than one inch. That is narrow escape number two, and Muffaroo just groans.

lady lovekins and old man mufferoo

A Story of Narrow Escapes is about
Lady Lovekins and Old Man Mufferoo.
Gustav Verbeek, *New York Herald,* circa 1900

9. "Oh, isn't he going to be cute," she cries, as the elephant rolls around, getting smaller and smaller until it is about the size of a dog.

4. Now this he should not have done, for the quick-eared elephant hears him and comes galloping up to see what is going on behind the trees. They are discovered! What is to be done?

8. "Come," says Lovekins, "let us watch him grow little."

5. Quick as a flash, Muffaroo hands the bottle to the elephant. The big fellow innocently sips the contents. He seems to like the stuff. That is narrow escape number three.

7. "That will settle him," says Old Man Muffaroo. "We need not be afraid now."

6. Lovekins and Muffaroo, peering out from the bushes, see him lie on his back in order to pour it down his throat more easily, for elephants cannot drink from bottles without lying on their backs.

Another Gustav Verbeek cartoon story about Lady Lovekins and Mufferoo, this one is called *The Fairy Palace*.

Gustav Verbeek, *New York Herald,* circa 1900

12. Then they climb down, more frightened than hurt, and run away, and Lovekins resolves never to give way to idle curiosity again.

1. One day Lovekins and Muffaroo come to a beautiful lake, just like a mirror. On the shore they see a lovely palace toward which they make their way.

11. He tosses them right through the door, into the branches of a palm tree outside.

2. "Let us go in!" cried little Lady Lovekins. Since the big door stands wide open, in they go.

10. Then a huge bull comes rushing out at them and tosses them with his horns.

3. Inside, a great genie floats up to them in a cloud of smoke. "You will find two mysterious closets," he says. "The one on the right you may open, but the left-hand one, open not! Oh, open not!"

9. The hobgoblins all at once slip back into their closet, because a terrible roaring now fills the whole palace. Lovekins and Muffaroo tremble.

4. Then he vanishes. Pretty soon they find the two mysterious closets. Muffaroo remembers the genie's words.

8. Instantly a hoard of loathsome hobgoblins come trooping out, and taking hold of our little heroes, they maul them and throw them up in the air.

5. So he opens only the right-hand door, and behold! Out come a lot of funny little fairies, singing sweet songs to them.

7. But when his back is turned, Lovekins quietly goes to the forbidden door on the left-hand side and opens it just enough for a tiny peek.

6. The fairies go back, and Muffaroo closes the door again. "I wonder what is in the other closet," says Lovekins. "And that we shall never know!" replies Old Man Muffaroo.

Here is the King. Where is the Queen?

Rex Whistler

This is a scary-looking old hag. Where is the young girl?
Rex Whistler

181 actress

Can you name this actress?

Answer: Marilyn Monroe

chapter 5

persistence of vision
(the afterimage)

Persistence of vision is as natural as breathing or ear wax. It happens all the time, but we ignore the process for the most part.

It is easy to 'see' afterimage illusions, even though they do not last long. The first thing to do is to stare at the illusion without moving your eyes. The idea is to 'charge up' or excite one group of sensors. If you move your eyes even a little, new sensors get excited and you will have to start over. How long should you stare? About 15-seconds will usually produce a fairly strong afterimage; generally the longer you stare, the stronger the afterimage, to a maximum of about 30-seconds.

Once your sensors are 'charged' shift your gaze to a blank space on a page or wall. A blank surface works well because it presents no 'new' distractions. As your eyes and sensors relax, the afterimage will appear on your retina. The illusion will seem to float and shift with eye movements before it quickly fades away.

You will discover an amazing thing about afterimages; they always occur up in the exact *opposite colour* of the original. A black image will produce a white afterimage; a red image will produce a green afterimage; blue, an orange afterimage; and so on. A full-colour negative would produce a normal full-colour picture in afterimage.

Some of the following afterimage illusions do not require 'charging' because they work while you are gazing at the figure. Have fun!

The white dots within the grid will appear to randomly flash in black as you gaze around the image. The black dots always seem to appear where you are not looking. If you look at them, they go away. They are real-time afterimages occurring where you have already looked.

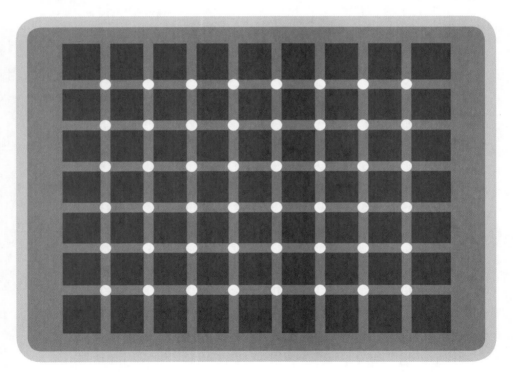

Here is a simple afterimage illusion to test your skills. Stare at the black dot on the left for a few seconds and then look at the centre of the square on the right. The afterimage that should develop will be of a floating fuzzy grey dot in the right hand square.

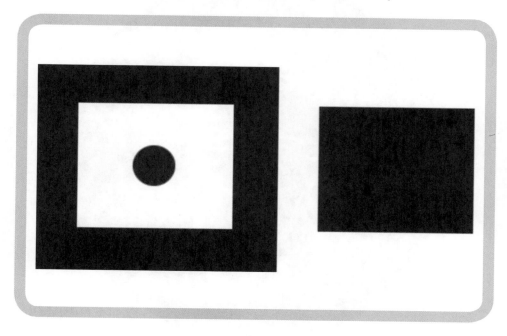

Celebrities have always been a favourite theme for afterimage illusions. The trick is to develop an afterimage and identify the famous person. Who is this famous pilot?

This famous person is known by many.

Answer: Jesus of Nazareth

Identify this famous revolutionary figure in afterimage.

Answer: Che Guevara

Who is this 'lighter-than-air' commander?

Can you identify this famous actress?

Answer: Greta Garbo

Can you identify this well-loved actress?

Answer: Greta Garbo

Can you name this U.S. president?

Answer: Thomas Jefferson

He was a famous leader during World War I. Can you name him?

Answer: Kaiser Wilhelm II

Illuminate this lightbulb with the power of your mind – and eye sensors.

In Shakespeare's play *Hamlet,* dead Yorick, who had once been a court jester, was represented by a bone white skull. Hamlet holds the cranium aloft and laments, 'Alas poor Yorick! I knew him well ...' To turn the famous skull white, you must first generate an afterimage.

Can you name this self-taught, rail-splitting U.S. president?

Answer: Abraham Lincoln

This is not a person but a famous painting. Can you name it?

Answer: The Mona Lisa by Leonardo da Vinci

Good-bye Norma Jean.
Can you name this actress?

Answer: Marilyn Monroe

This U.S. president was sometimes called 'Tricky Dickie'.
Can you name him?

Answer: Richard Milhous Nixon

This U.S. president promised 'change.'
Can you name him?

Answer: Barack Obama

This is the first African-American president.
Can you name him?

Answer: Barack Obama

As you stare at this design, ghostly afterimage 'particles' will begin to swirl and race around the circles.

Give this image a fixed stare for a few seconds and then move your eyes slightly. White dots will appear among the black.

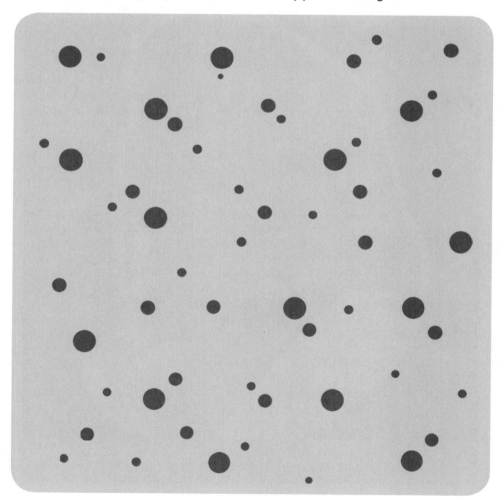

Can you name this British monarch?

Answer: Queen Victoria

Can you name this U.S. president?

Answer: Franklin D. Roosevelt

Can you name this U.S. president?

Answer: George Washington

Name this GOP presidential candidate from 1940.

Answer: Wendell Wilkie

206 100-point star

This geometric shape is actually a distorted star with 100 points. The geometry causes a contrast illusion in the bright ring, where the spokes are narrow. The bright white colour in the ring is the same as the white colour anywhere else. It just looks brighter!

chapter 6

contrast anomalies

The word *contrast*, in this context means 'to compare'; to contrast one thing against the other. We are all masters in the art of contrast. We compare everything with everything else. In a big way, this is how we navigate in three dimensions. We especially like to contrast or compare colours.

Colours affect us in ways that we can see and accept. We describe them anthropomorphically with words, such as hot, cool, warm, and soothing, and most of us will have a favourite colour in mind. Nations go to war under national colours. Colours can also affect us in small ways that we cannot easily see. Contrast illusions are perfect for visualizing small quirks in our vigorous habit of comparing hues.

Every colour affects every other colour nearby. If you put a lot of light colour next to a little bit of dark colour, the dark colour will 'look' lighter than it really is. Artists have used this secret for centuries very effectively. A cat breeder once said that to have a cat which is truly white – get two black cats as well.

To make contrast illusions work, all you have to do is look at them; the effect is fully automatic – like breathing. Birds have to sing; we have to compare. You will be amazed at the things you might see that aren't really there.

The centre of the Burning Fuse Illusion appears zapped in white heat. The centre is not brighter, it is an illusion caused by the dark cross ramping down to meet in the centre. You might also see a darker 'halo' around the centre. This is dark colour 'bleeding' into open areas from the cross.

Illustration by Arthur Azevedo

In this variation of the Burning Fuse illusion, the centre of the crossbeams is not really brighter than the white of the page. It only looks so – in contrast.

This star shape has so many points that they melt into a mist. There is also a curious moiré pattern that forms within the shape.

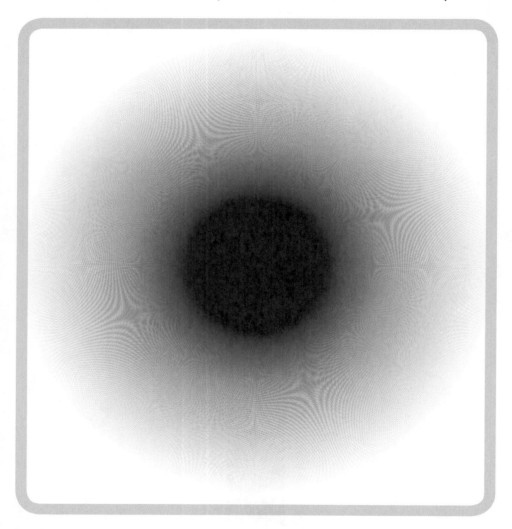

Here is another geometric pattern with a contrast illusion. The white colour in the centre is not brighter than any other white colour nearby.

Here is an elegant example of a contrast illusion.
The grey dots are identical in colour and hue.

The Cornsweet Illusion is an excellent example of colour bleeding. Both halves of the figure are identical in colour and hue. The left appears darker because colour is bleeding over the left-hand side from just the tiny shadow line down the centre. Cover the tiny shadow line with your finger, pencil, or strip of paper and you will see that the areas on either side of the centre are identical.

The Flashing Dots Illusion is more than just an afterimage illusion; it's also a contrast illusion. The white dots look brighter because they each have a huge amount of black nearby. This enhances the afterimage illusion. The dots will flash on and off as you gaze at the figure.

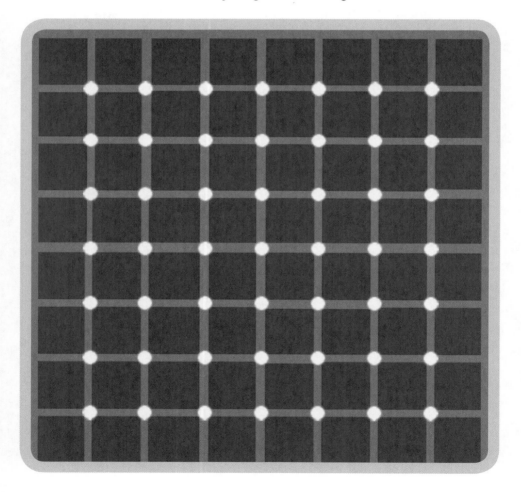

The Doughnuts on a Tablecloth is an experiment in contrast. The doughnuts are all the same; the idea is to see how the random shades of grey in the background affect how they appear.

Here is another exploration of the Doughnuts on a Tablecloth illusion.

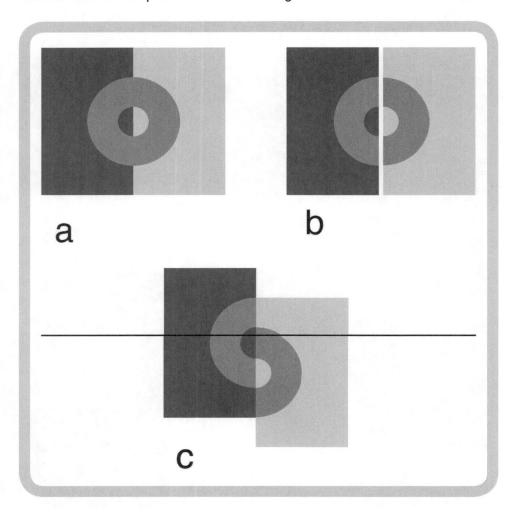

The columns and rows of black and white dashes create contrast havoc on the neutral grey background in this figure.

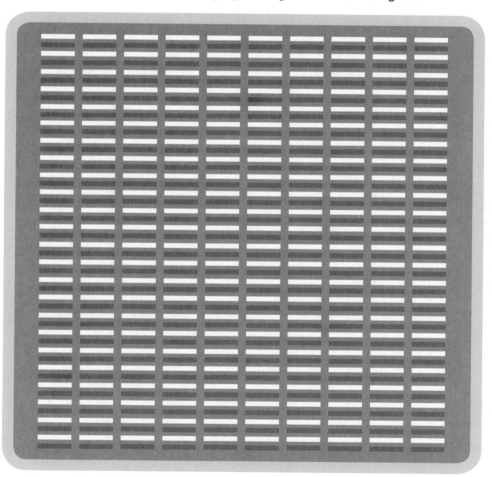

This variation of the Burning Fuse Illusion (see page 222) creates the same effect in a grid pattern.

Illustration by Arthur Azevedo

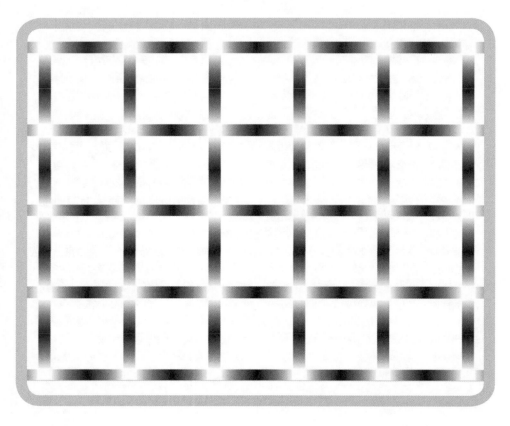

Here is a another variation of the Burning Fuse Effect (see page 222).
Illustration by Arthur Azevedo

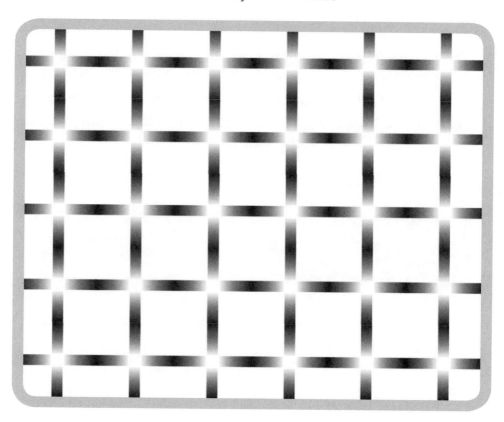

The background in this figure is graduated 50 per cent grey on the left to 100 per cent white on the right. The horizontal bar running through the centre is one shade of grey. It is easy to see colour influence as we compare the bar along its length to the 'ramping' hue in the background.

There are only three hues in this design, although it looks like there are four. Can you identify the 'extra' illusory hue in this figure?

See the answer on page 372.

This design for a greeting card shows the effects of contrast on identical hearts within different background hues.

This example presents a little powerhouse of contrast. The chunky bit of chequerboard is uniform, with alternating squares of light and dark hues. A grey column casts a shadow across the board. Compare square (A) with square (B). Yes, they're the same hue! The squares around (B) are darker because they are in shadow – they make (B) look lighter. Square (A) is mostly surrounded by light squares – these squares make (A) look darker. The two contrast illusions combined to create a single phantasy in contrast.

Original design: R. Beau Lotto

The Laura's Eyes Illusion will sometimes appear with open eyes, and sometimes closed.

This is a contrast illusion using the contrast illusion Laura's Eyes. Identical Laura's are contrasted against a wash of background hues. Interestingly, the Laura's Eyes illusion seems to work even here.

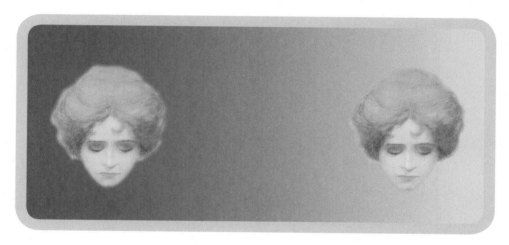

mccourt effect

This figure, is an artful variation on background influence.
The bar going across is all one single hue of grey.

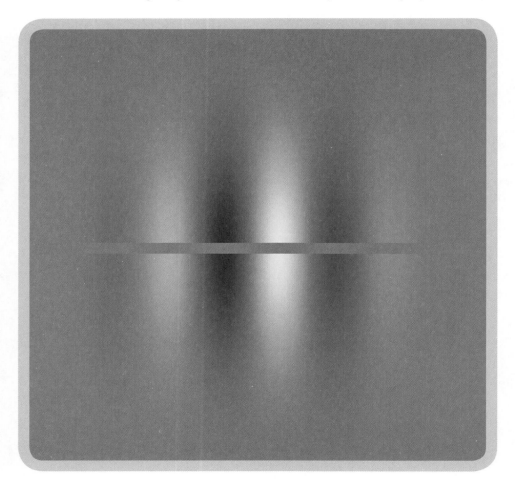

The so-called Ouchi Illusion demonstrates a dazzling contrast effect. As you stare at the figure, the background pattern will tend to separate and shimmer beneath the circle in the foreground.

Here is another version of the Ouchi Illusion (see page 241) with similar effects.

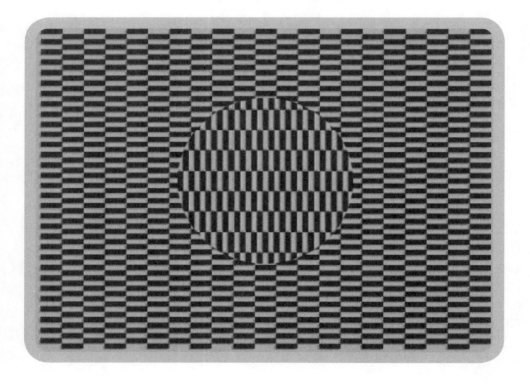

In the Pin Stripe Illusion, the grey hue is the same throughout the figure. Black influences the inner square and white rules the large square.

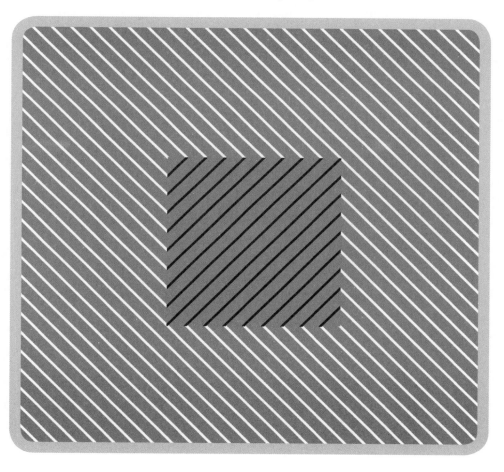

Each pair of dashes are identical in hue. Each background regulates a dashed pair's appearance with a contrast illusion.

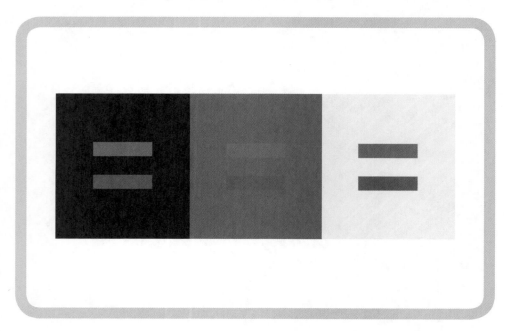

The Ten Per Cent Illusion goes from 100 per cent white to 100 per cent black in ten steps. The centre bar is 50 per cent black throughout.

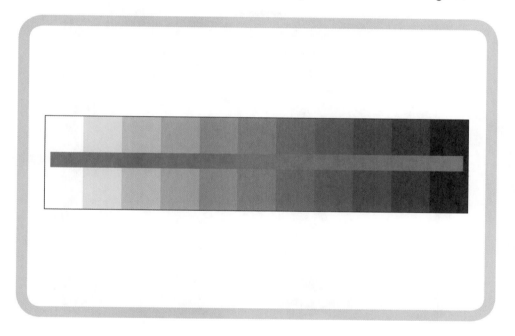

The white tape holding these drums together is all one hue.

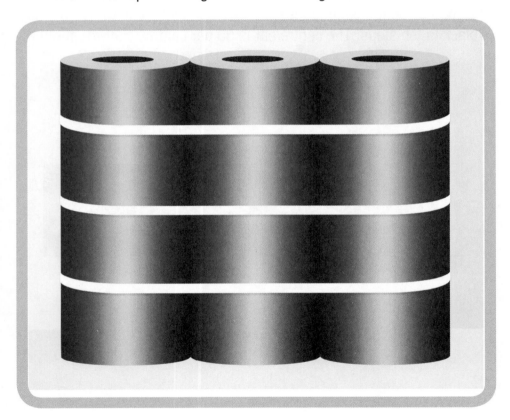

Because of contrast it is easy to imagine that the black rectangle is behind a translucent grey square. Or it's just three shapes. Or the black square is magnifying the grey square underneath. Or…

Here is a variation of the Pin Stripe Illusion (see page 243).

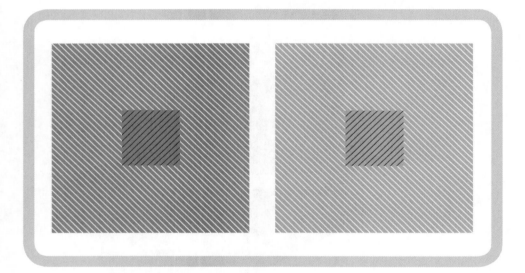

In this figure the black dots will flash white as you look at the image.

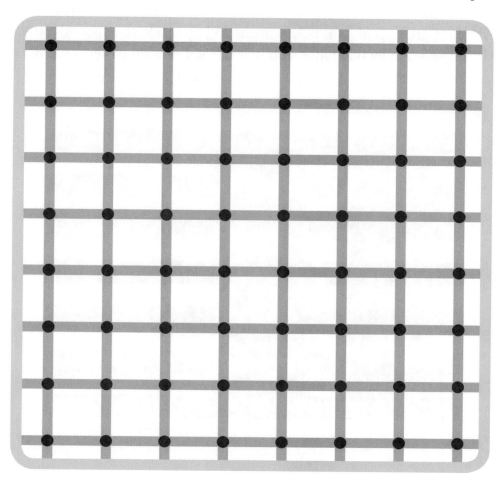

The grey panels are all the same hue in the Woven Bar illusion. The first grey panel is mostly surrounded by black; the second panel is surrounded by half white and half black; the third panel is mostly surrounded by white. Each panel is contrasted differently.

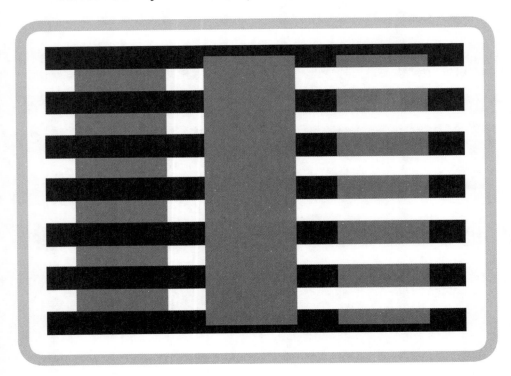

In this illusion the X's look like they are different hues, even though they are solidly connected.

237 tri-bar in the clouds

Here is an impossible object with a lot of different illusions.

chapter 7

impossible objects

Impossible objects are, well, impossible, meaning they cannot exist in our three-dimensional world. Impossible objects can only exist on paper. They are pictures drawn to look three-dimensional and mimic real-life three-dimensional objects. Impossible renderings inspire us to take a second look, and then we notice that something is wrong. Something about the geometry is half-twisted from real.

We are masters of three dimensions and we each carry a built-in sense of what looks right. It may be partly for this reason that we love impossible objects. Seeing something that looks real, but is an oddity, a chink in the foundation of our sense of right, can be an enchanting experience.

Every figure in this chapter is impossible in one way or another. Many individual parts of these objects may look perfectly normal, but one flaw makes the whole impossible. Find out how some impossible objects can escape the world of flat paper and exist in the world of three dimensions. Get ready to explore the impossible!

The Impossible Triangle, or Triad or sometimes the Tri-bar illusion, is the simplest most elegant impossible object anyone has ever designed. Oscar Reutersvärd created the world's first triad design. Roger Penrose, cofounder of the Big Bang Theory, called the triad design, 'Impossibility in its purest form.'

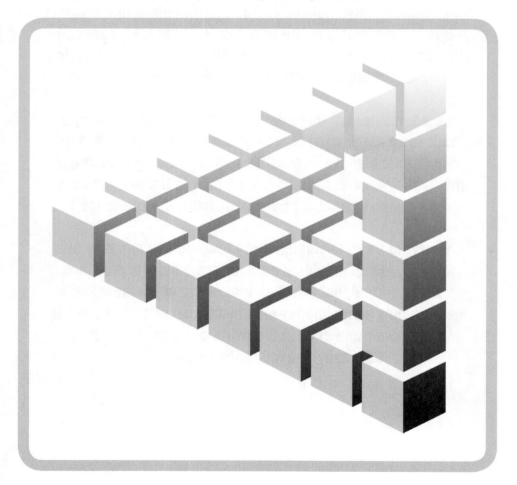

This variation of the impossible Triangle design is made from identical blocks. There are two sides with seven blocks and one side with six blocks. Hey! That's impossible.

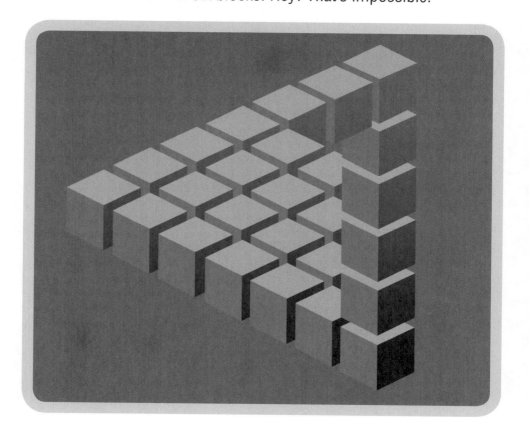

An impossible square design set in a
gloopy alien landscape.

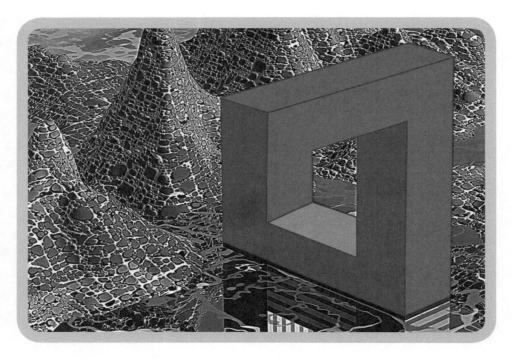

In the Bent Pencil Illusion, unless the pencil is rubberized,
it cannot bend this way.

Rigid rectangles on the table cannot bend this way, and this one isn't either. It just looks that way. It's impossible.

Three rugged and rigid rings can certainly link up in this way,
but they can't lie flat like this. It's impossible.

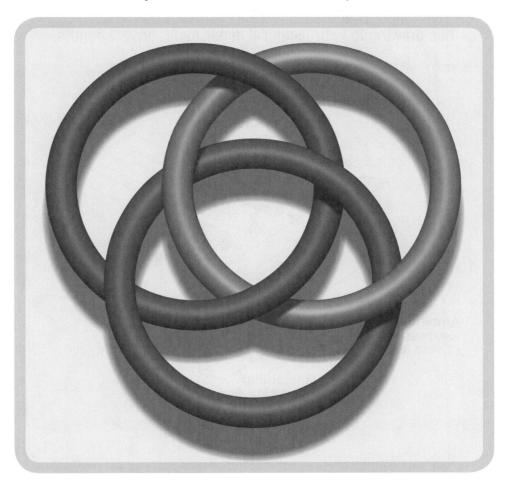

This schematic contains three impossible hexnuts, one impossible square, and a threaded Devil's Fork (see page 264). Give this drawing to your technical department; drive 'em nuts.

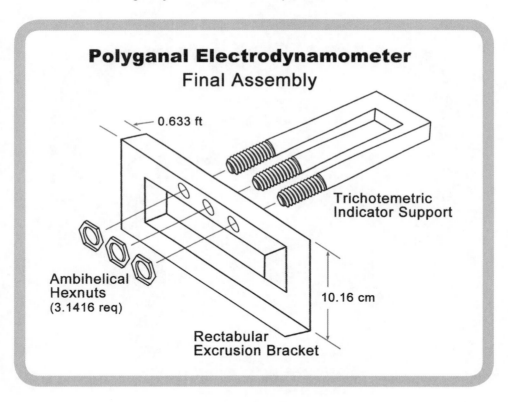

Polyganal Electrodynamometer
Final Assembly

0.633 ft

Trichotemetric
Indicator Support

Ambihelical
Hexnuts
(3.1416 req)

10.16 cm

Rectabular
Excrusion Bracket

Both ends of the board seem to face forward and the chess pieces are hanging every which way; this game is going to last impossibly long.

No matter how fast and how far you climb, you will never get anywhere on this stairway. The staircase goes endless up or endlessly down.

A resort offers this new water sports feature, but people are complaining. The stairs don't go anywhere – except to the same level!

In the Classic Devil's Fork, or Trident Illusion, it starts out a solid rectangle and ends up a threaded round fork.

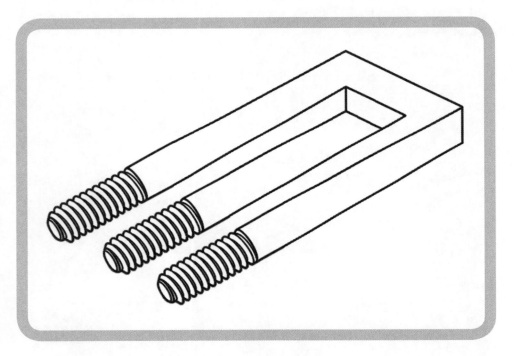

A variation of the Devil's Fork design (see opposite page).

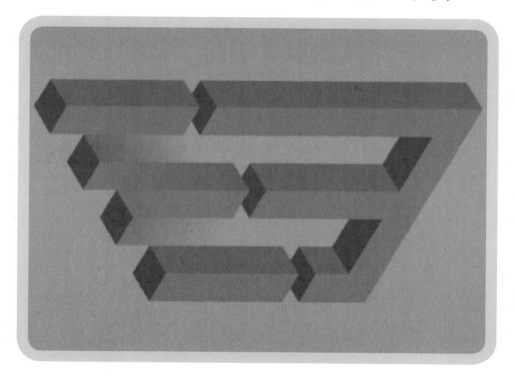

Faux Escalier, or False Stairs is an illustrated impossible stair design.

These three gears cannot work. Places where the gears
mesh are hopelessly twisted. The gears 'share' contours and
could not exist alone. They could not turn either.

This 18th century drawing by artist William Hogarth
has many things wrong with it. How many can you find?

In this homage to Sandro Del-Prête, the wheel
can never do any work.
Original design by Sandro Del-Prête, *Quadrature of the Wheel*

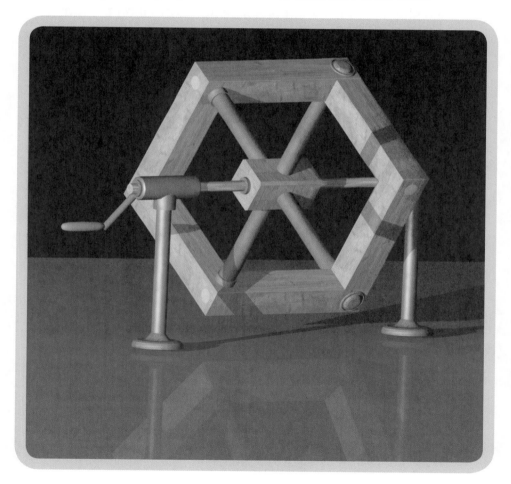

These steps are hollow on one side and normal on the other.
It's impossible!

These three blocks cannot fit together as they are pictured.
What's wrong?

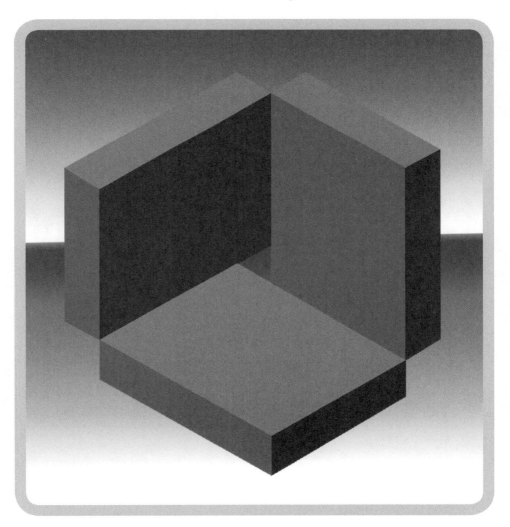

This outdoor sculpture looks impossible from one single viewing angle. If you look at it from any other angle, it looks like three arms going off in different directions. Within this narrow parameter impossible objects can exist!

East Perth, Western Australia

This ticket booth is impossible. If you see one of these at the fair, run back to your spaceship – you are not on planet earth!

This impossible form looks okay until ... you get to the vertical bar on the front.

A salute to Oscar Reutersvärd, creator of the world's first impossible triangle design in 1934.

Original design by Oscar Reutersvärd, *Opus 1,* 1934

This outdoor sculpture is only impossible from this unique viewpoint. Any other viewing angle will reveal the actual shape of the beams.

Impossible Sculpture, Gotschuchen, Austria

The Möbius strip is not impossible, but it acts in a way similar to an impossible object. A Möbius strip can be made out of any long strip of paper. Before gluing the ends together, twist the strip exactly one-half turn. Follow any surface or edge around the Möbius and you will end up where you started.

Pencils can intertwine like this, but not as shown. It's impossible.

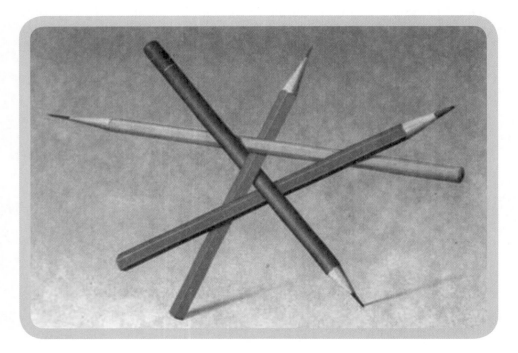

These pairs of pizza pie slices cannot fit together in this way. Why?

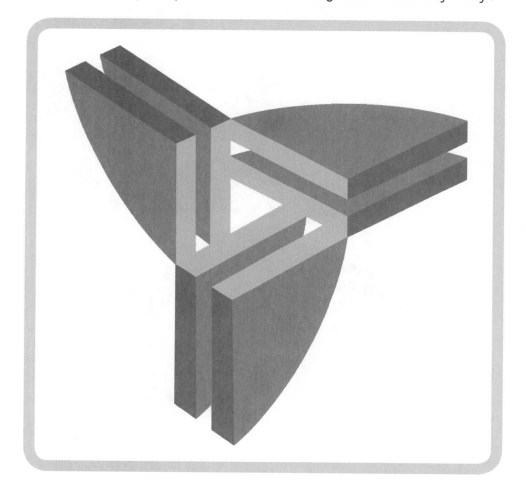

This design for a Tinkertoy would not be found in a toy shop.

Here is another impossible design, this one for a bird box.

Not many people would stack wood as shown here.

A cube may be dissected in this way, but it would never look like this.

The image on the canvas is an extension of the scene in the doorway.

It's unlikely you'll come across a tree like this in nature.

Here is a design for an impossible cube.

A storm has left an impossible rectangle on the beach.

Camouflage

1

2 3 4 5 6 7 8 9 0 1   2 3 4 5 6 >

272 **cheetah and a barcode sticker**

This graphic design uses a symbol of industry to
demonstrate an odd method of camouflage.

chapter 8

camouflage

The word *camouflage* comes from an old Parisian slang term, *camoufler*, meaning 'to disguise.' During World War I, *camouflage* described anything that was 'hidden in plain sight' by using war paint, special clothing, camouflage nets, deceitful patterns, or even natural terrain. Nowadays, the term applies to all of nature as well.

A useful camouflage pattern breaks up the visible properties of an object, and confuses a stalking predator. The object and background become indistinguishable. If you live where there is a lot of green, it helps if you are green, too. If hungry predators can't find you, they can't eat you. You will live to have more green offspring, who will survive because you passed on your greenness. Camouflage is Nature's pledge to favour those who survive.

Natural camouflage is not a choice; no bug decides to look like a leaf or a twig. The process takes millions of years, powered by the unwavering march of natural selection. There is also something called unnatural selection. Garden peas did not decide to become sweet-flavoured. Millions of years of creatures choosing – eating – and excreting only the sweetest peas produced the dulcet pea we know. In concert with nature and greedy appetites, animals unconsciously nurture a variety of tasty foods.

Get ready to sample some of our favourite examples of natural and man-made camouflage illusions. How good are you at spotting a prey, seeing through the leafy clutter, or tracking down a hidden quarry? Do you have 'hunters' eyes? Get ready to hack your way through the tangled world of camouflage illusions.

This photograph has been rigged to remove some the details and all of the colour except black and white. Can you spot all six zebras in the photo? If you were a hungry lion, this is pretty close to what you would see … better lie low and wait for something to move.

This photograph from World War I shows the troop ship *Prince of Wales* fully camouflagued in razzle dazzle paint. Camouflage patterns weren't meant to hide a ship, but rather to confuse an enemy observer. An observer, after spotting the ship must quickly report her exact position, course and speed. (This was before radar.) A camouflaged ship matches the colour of the sky and sports large dark and confusing shapes. Lacking visual clues, the observer cannot easily tell if the ship is coming towards him or going away. By the time he figures it out, the *Prince of Wales* could be over the horizon – safely beyond range.

What is hidden in this camouflaged pattern?

Can you find a spotted white cat in this wintry scene?

See the answer on page 372.

This graphic design hides a fast hunter.
Can you find a speeding cheetah?

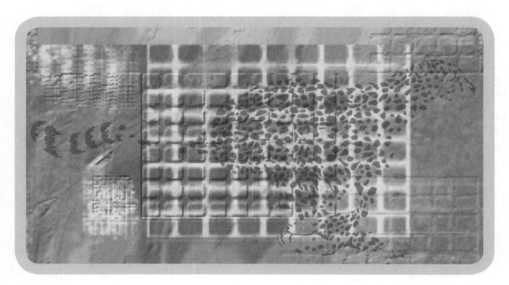

To camouflage this picture, much of the visual information has been removed. Are there enough clues left for you to identify what is pictured?

See the answer on page 372.

What do you see here?

See the answer on page 373.

Sometimes the best camouflage is to clam up, and act like you belong. Can you spot the quarry?

'Become the leaf Grasshopper.'
Can you spot the camouflaged bug?

This leaf-shaped moth is well suited to its environment.

Can you find the leaf-mimicking bug in this photo?

Find a leaf-mimicking frog in the leafy litter. It isn't easy to find this little fellow. He's small and looks just like everything else.

See the answer on page 373.

This frog is well camouflaged in its own habitat.
Can you spot him?

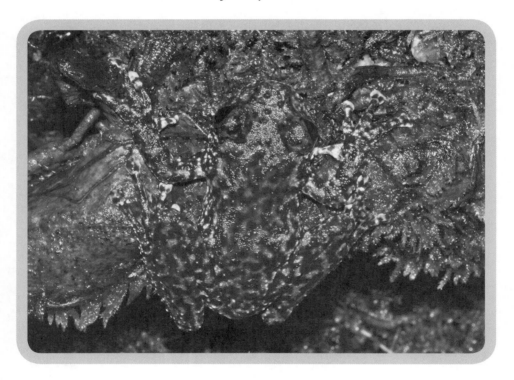

A U.S. Marine stands guard in Afghanistan. His uniform and equipment are decorated in dusty camouflage patterns appropriate for this environment.

The small twig on top of the branch is the spider.

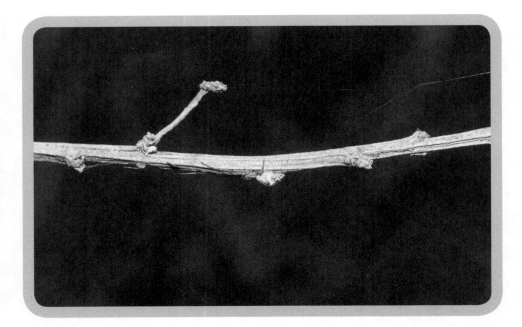

These guys are perfectly camouflaged in their native Australian habitat. If they sit still, you can't tell them from bark.

289 the ambassadors

Two French Ambassadors are pictured in the painting; Jean de Dinteville, and Georges de Selve. The picture is also filled with symbols; the broken flute, an odd assortment of tools, instruments, etc. The distorted shape near the bottom of the painting is an anamorphic illusion. To find out what it is you must look at in the right way.

Painting by Hans Holbein the Younger

See the answer on page 373.

chapter 9

miscellaneous
illusions
anamorphic changelings

Anamorphosis, when applied to illusory figures, means to change, to evolve or change into something all-together different when you look at the image in the right way. Anamorphic illusions often have hidden messages, or aspects that can be revealed. In order to solve an anamorphic puzzle, one must tilt, rotate, or do a combination of both. There are even some anamorphic images which can only be revealed on a mirrored cylinder; of course, we all have one of those lying around.

Leonardo da Vinci, who spent much of his time designing weapons, filled many of his journals with strange nonsensical handwriting. The text was later discovered to be Leonardo's own code – an anamorphic illusion. The text could only be deciphered by using a mirror. The great inventor/artist must have been worried about industrial espionage over 400 years ago.

A fascinating and easy anamorphic puzzle to solve, no matter how you look at it you always see another face! This image is also special because it is made entirely of capital letters. To see this anamorphic changeling clearly, stand off a bit and look at it.

Here is an example of a relatively new art form known as ASCII Art. The art form is named for the American Standard Code for Information Interchange, an encoding scheme used for computer text characters. The picture is made entirely of capital letters. To view this anamorphic illusion, stand back away and look at it. When you see it clearly, Laura's eyes may appear both open and closed.

This old cartoon's caption reads, 'Find the Bridegroom.' Sadly, the answer, if there ever was one, is missing. We haven't been able to find the bridegroom! Does he really exist? Will you be the first to find him? Good luck!

Here is an anamorphic illusion that is also an advertising card for a Victorian garment retailer. The way to reveal the illusion is to stare at the vertical line in the centre while slowly drawing the image closer to your eyes. The two halves will merge in the mind's eye and the lady will model the merchandise.

Stare at the centre of this image and gently cross your eyes until the two images merge to complete the design.

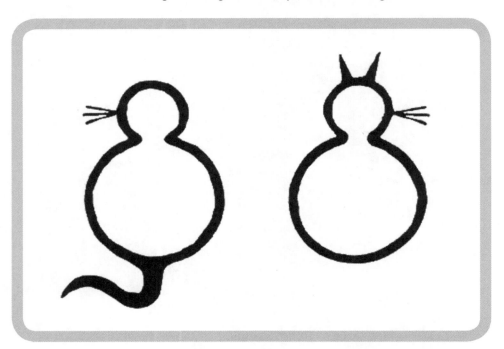

Find the hidden face in this drawing.

Answer: Rotate the image 90 degrees anti-clockwise.
The face is in the centre of the image.

This graphic design hides a message that is also a palindrome. A palindrome is a special kind of sentence that reads the same forward and backward. To reveal the message, you must view the image in the correct way. Try rotating the image 90 degrees clockwise and then tilt the top of the image away from you drastically.

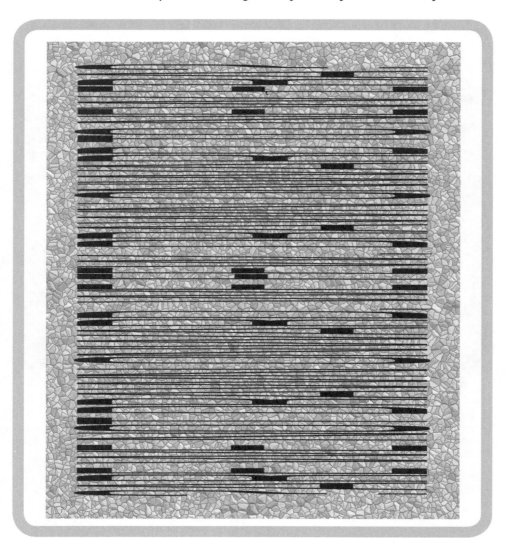

Answer: Are we not drawn onward, we few,
drawn onward to new era?

This anamorphic message is a very simple, one word. Tilt the top of the image away from you until you can read the message.

The way to view this picture of Christ is to shake the image slightly or move it back and forth.

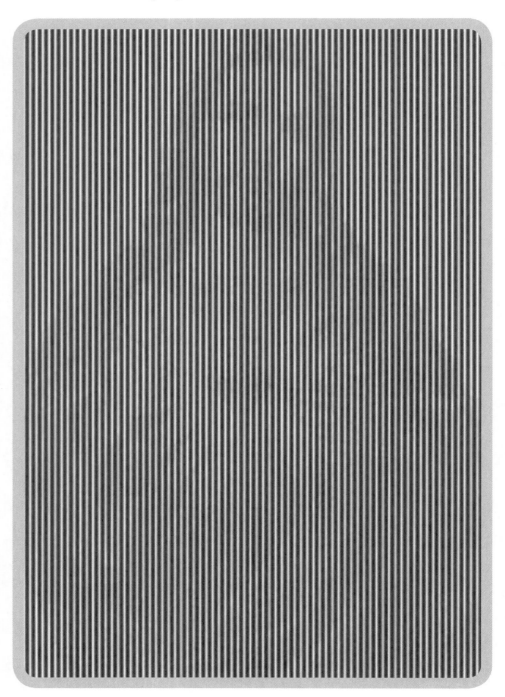

Find a way to view this image so that the spikes stand up
and look sort like a three-dimensional sprig of sticks.

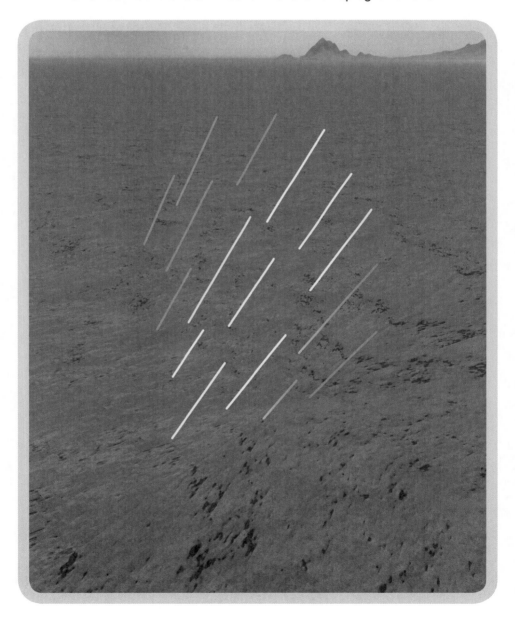

Find a sword, a wizard, a horse and a joker in this handsome sketch.

See the answer on page 374.

Can you find all four of the dinosaurs hidden in this drawing?

See the answer on page 374.

Tilt the top of the image away from you until the message becomes readable. The message is also a palindrome, a word or phrase that reads the same forward and backward.

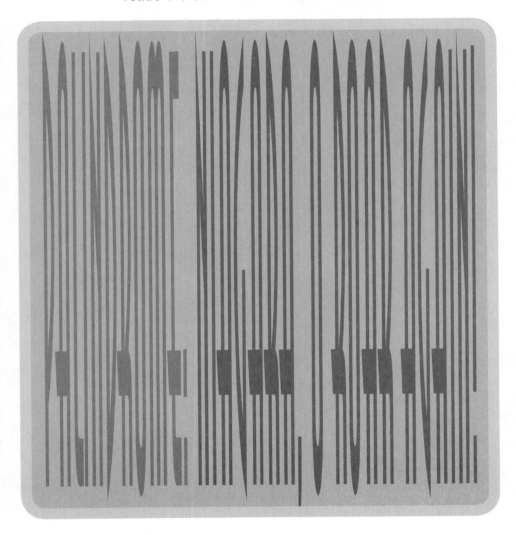

Answer: PALINDROME: NIAGARA, O ROAR AGAIN.

Here is another anamorphic puzzle that is also two palindromes (see opposite page). Tilt the top of the image away from you to reveal the message.

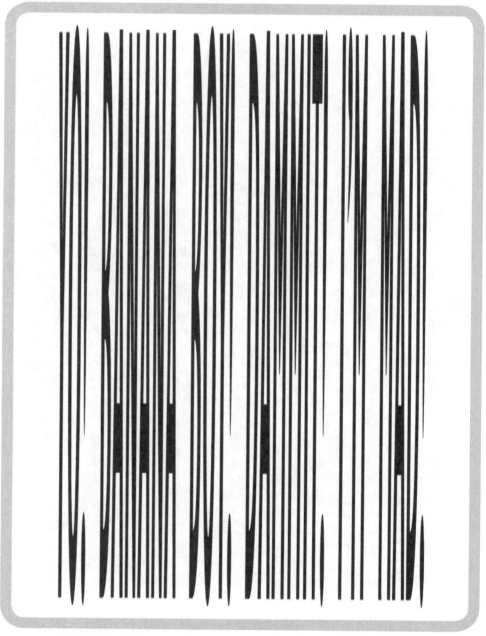

Answer: Ref – YO! BANANA BOY! and DAMMIT! I'M MAD!

Can you find the Old Women in this picture puzzle?

See the answer on page 374.

This delightful drawing has so many hidden animals that it is hard to count them all! How many can you find?

See the answer on page 375.

This design for a Christmas card has two hidden greetings.
Can you decipher them both?

Answers: MERRY CHRISTMAS! and HAVE A HAPPY NEW YEAR!

This old Valentine's Day card has an anamorphic message.
Can you decipher Cupid's message?

Answer: LOVE ME LITTLE, LOVE ME LONG

When should a pretty girl be hugged?
Can you work out the answer in this anamorphic changeling?

Answer: **WHEN DANGEROUS CIRCUMSTANCES REQUIRE HER TO BE 'ARMED.'**

What are women so wicked?
Solve the anamorphic puzzle to find the answer.

Why are women
so wicked?
(find the answer)

Answer: BECAUSE THEY STEEL THEIR CORSETS, CRIB THEIR BABIES,
AND HOOK ONE ANOTHER'S DRESSES.

310 **spinning wheels**

Keeping your eyes moving around this figure will generate a double dose of apparent motion.

From original designs by Akiyoshi Kitaoka

chapter 10

miscellaneous illusions
apparent motion

Sometimes objects on a two-dimensional surface can appear like they are moving when they are really not. Apparent movement illusions have to do with comparative contrast and afterimages – the fact that a picture tends to linger on the retina for a very short, but existent time.

Sometimes a movement will generate in real time, and will be visible only when our eyes are moving naturally around the figure. When we focus on one spot, our visual processors kick into high gear and work to steady the image. Other variations of the effects require a more physical approach, such as moving towards or away from the image while you are looking at it.

Even though we know that all two-dimensional movement is illusory outside of a motion picture screen, it is thrilling to see the effects in real time. Get ready to take in some illusionary movement from the comfort of your armchair.

This figure generates a rippling effect. Keep your eyes moving!
Did you notice that the little squares have black and white edges?
These edges are powering the effect. The direction of apparent
movement is based on which side is white or black.

From original designs by Akiyoshi Kitaoka

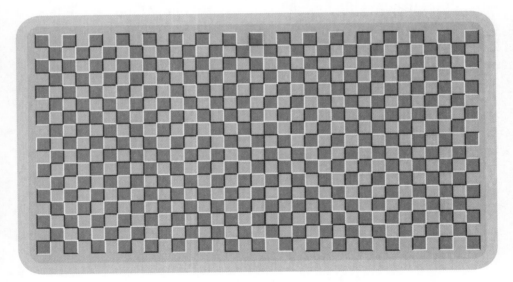

This high-tech drawing may appear to bulge as you gaze into its metallic countenance.

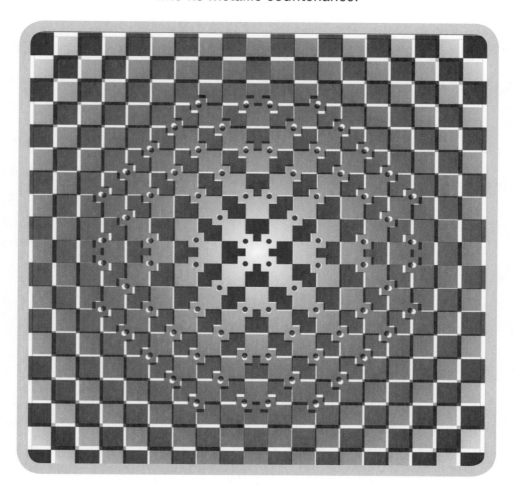

This variation ripples back and forth in long rows.
Do white edges on the oval shapes point in the direction of
movement? What do you think?

From original designs by Akiyoshi Kitaoka

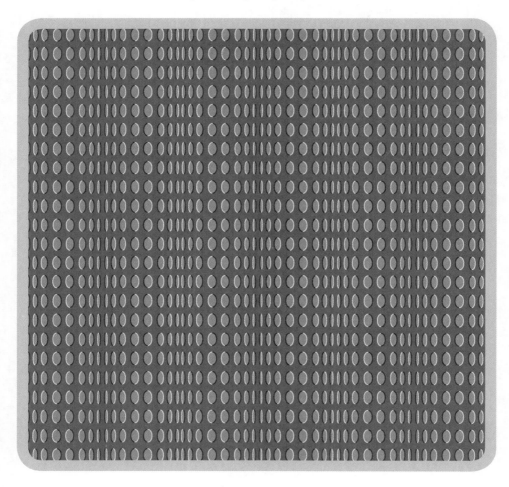

Something is rustling under this pile of leaflike objects.
Keep your eyes moving to see illusory motion over the entire image.

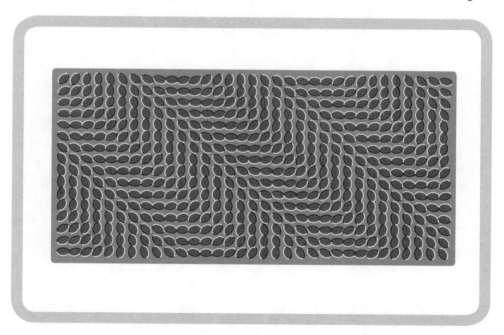

Keep your eyes moving to see the rotating effect of
this contrasting circle design.

From original designs by Akiyoshi Kitaoka

Here is another rotating effect.

From original designs by Akiyoshi Kitaoka

To see rotating motion in this illusion, hold the image at arm's length with both hands and then move it closer to your eyes as you look at it. Continue the illusory movement by moving the image slowly away again.

Illustration by Arthur Azevedo

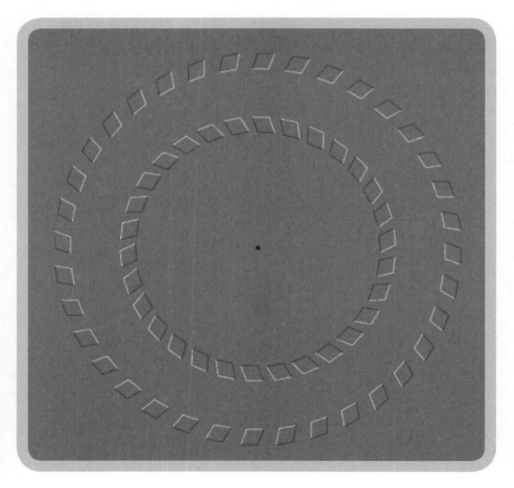

To see rotating motion in this illusion, hold the image at arm's length with both hands and then move it closer to your eyes as you look at it. Continue the illusory movement by moving the image slowly away again.

Illustration by Arthur Azevedo

To see rotating motion in this illusion, hold the image at arm's length with both hands and then move it closer to your eyes as you look at it. Continue the illusory movement by moving the image slowly away again.

Illustration by Arthur Azevedo

To see rotating motion in this illusion, hold the image at arm's length with both hands and then move it closer to your eyes as you look at it. Continue the illusory movement by moving the image slowly away again.

Illustration by Arthur Azevedo

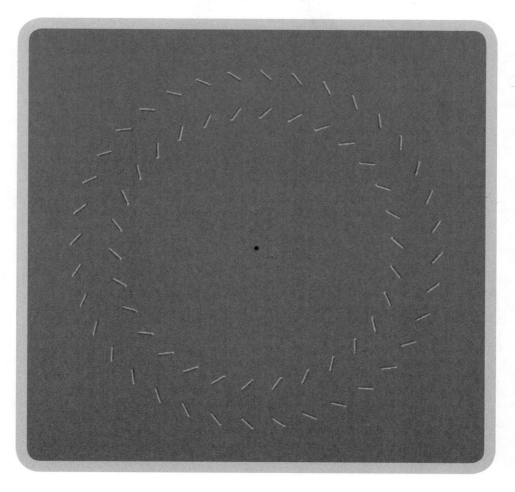

321 tsunami hazard sign

Tsunami Hazard Sign: This international hazard sign for tsunami was recently approved. We can all see the wave, yet part of it is a subjective illusion.

chapter 11

miscellaneous illusions
subjective phantoms

Subjective illusions do not exist, except in the mind's eye. We see them clearly, but they exist only because of another object or objects in an image. They are bound to and *subject* to the existence of the other object(s). If you want to attack the examples here with an eraser, you don't need to scrub the subjective illusions; as everything else goes, they would cease to exist.

In this subjective phrase, the words CAST SHADOW do not exist.
The illusion is merely empty space shaped like the words. If you
remove the drop shadow, the words will disappear.

These funny looking signs are hiding a secret word, which
is also a subjective illusion. Can you solve the puzzle? Remember to
see what isn't there!

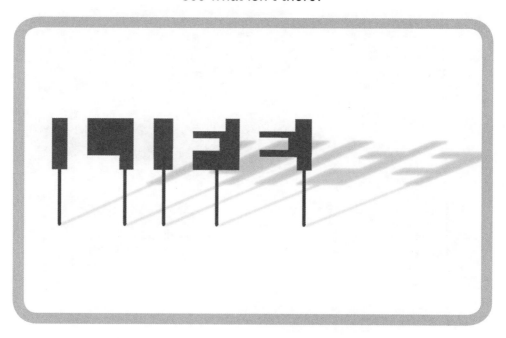

The three Pacman shapes help nurture the idea that a
solid pyramid is floating between them. The far walls and corner are
colluding to create the illusion.

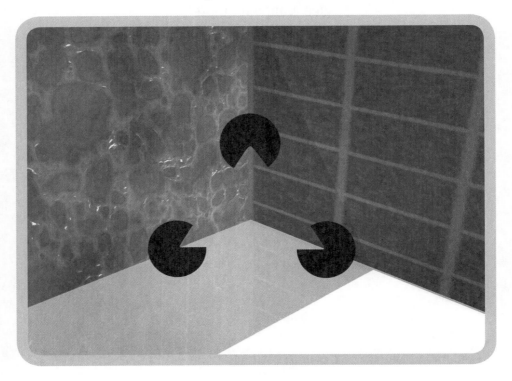

Three Pacman shapes define a three-pointed star illusion in this Kanisaw Illusion. So real is the illusory star that we can easily imagine the curve of the points within the empty spaces.

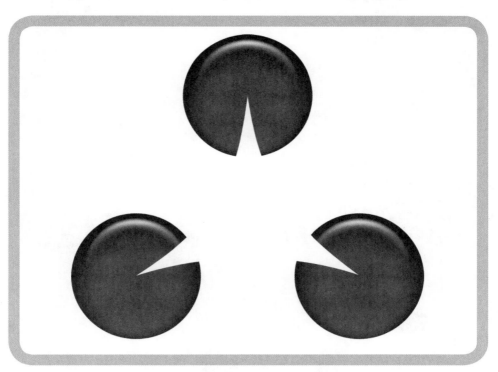

Find the subjective lightbulb in this subjective hidden picture.

See the answer on page 375.

These eight gel buttons are fixing some of the features of the famous Necker Cube. Can you visualize the entire wire-framed cube?

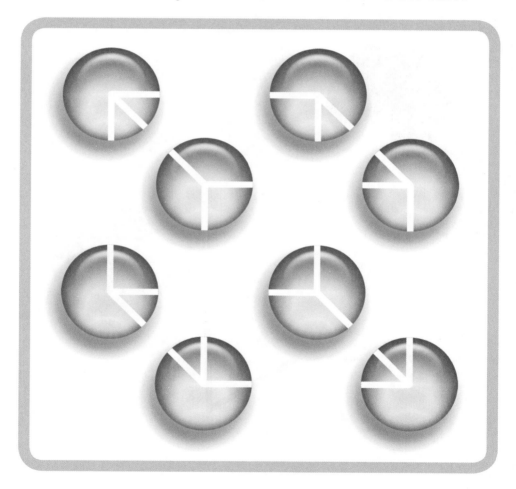

See the answer on page 375.

Three Pacman shapes define a subjective triangle, which, in turn, helps to define a six-point star design.

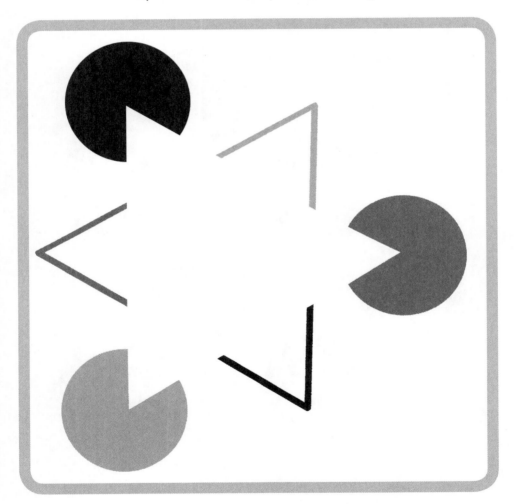

In this design the circle shape is subjective and is defined by line segments, which are painted white. We can also see that the subjective circle is lighter in colour and has definite borders inside and out. This is an illusion; there are no borders or a lighter colour.

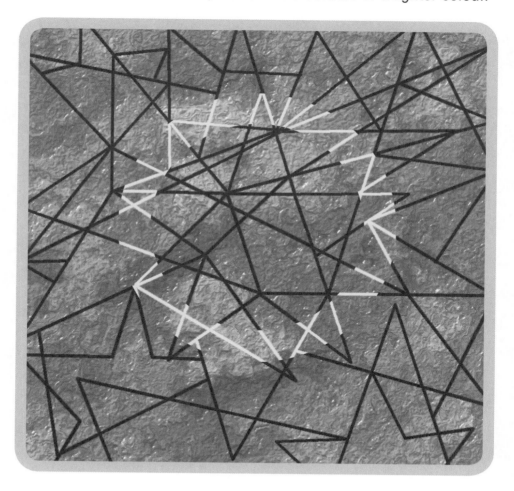

Six sailboats in a circle define a subjective flower
shape in the centre. Can you see it?

Can you find a wine glass in this hodgepodge of miscellaneous shapes?

See the answer on page 376.

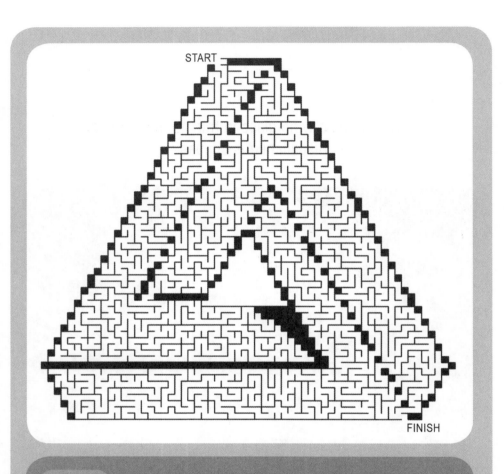

START

FINISH

332 impossible object and maze illusion

The Impossible Object and Maze Illusion. Follow the maze through an impossible triangle.

See the answer on page 376.

chapter 12

puzzles

What book about illusions and puzzles would be complete without actual puzzles? You will find illusion-related mazes, word searches, and many other puzzles. You can even learn to draw your own illusions! Here are some of our favourite puzzles and games for the pencil-wise and the curious.

333 ballerina maze

In the Ballerina Maze and distortion illusion, the two ballerinas are identical and level, yet the dancer on the right appears loftier and somehow different. The illusion is accomplished by simply dropping one of the drop shadows down a bit.

See the answer on page 376.

The Mind Reader game will divine your thoughts.
Start by checking out the current hand of six cards shown here.
Pick one of the cards and memorize it; so this book can get a clear
mental reading from you. Ready? Now turn the page…

Carefully scan the hand again, shown here. Is your card missing? Is this the world's first mind-reading book, or a devious trick?

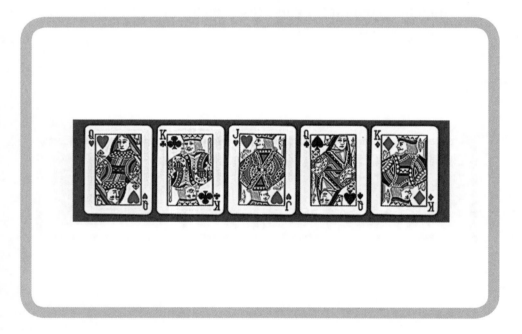

Answer: The second hand is completely different from the first. This book will read your mind no matter which card you choose from the first hand.

In the Ten Cats Illusion and Maze, first find all ten cats in the illustration, then enjoy a romp through the maze.

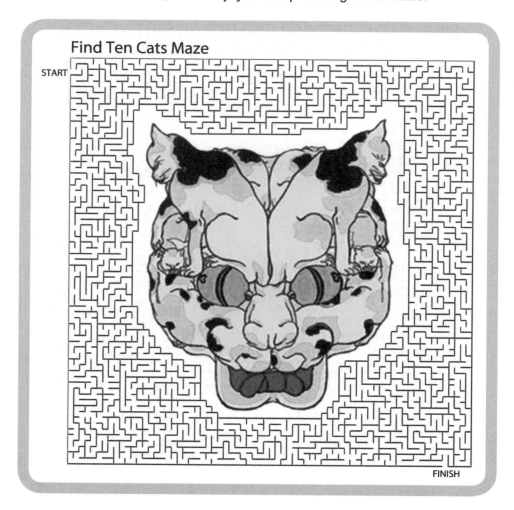

See the answer on page 377.

A visiting monk has misplaced his twin brother. Help find the missing twin, and then solve a double dose of mazes.

See the answer on page 377.

Answer: Turn the image upside down to find the missing twin.

The Devil's Fork design is an impossible object. Let's hope the maze isn't impossible. Follow the strings through the maze.

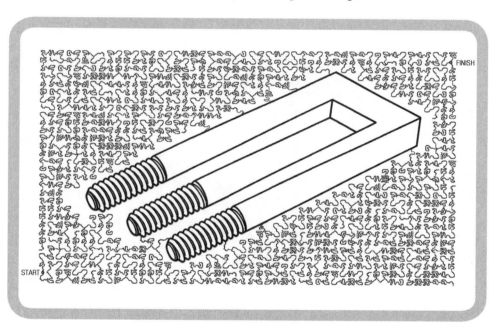

See the answer on page 377.

Find the words in the puzzle list within the matrix of letters.
Words can be found oriented up, down, perpendicular, or reversed.

```
J W Q T L R Y N E Y D E W C G O
W S U O U G I B M A R T P T W T
E V I T I U T N I R E T N U O C
H L E L B A T S N U V Z W I O E
L X E G S S E L D N E Z I M X F
J V P P A V R B R Y R Z P P D F
C R E N J M B X E Q S L X O F E
O C W C P H I T A U I W D S K R
T Y D M A H S R D M B F H S L E
E A J W A A A K E P L I Q I U T
B L Z U R A M N R T E E E B R F
J B B T M Z T O T J F G W L Z A
W G N I G A L F U O M A C E M I
N O I T R O T S I D M R P H U X
C L A Y C A J Z A F J I Q M A R
R T K I N V N O I T O M I F F B
```

AFTEREFFECT	COMPLIMENTARY	MINDREADER
AFTERIMAGE	CONTRAST	MIRAGE
AMBIGUOUS	COUNTERINTUITIVE	MOTION
ASPECT	DISTORTION	PHANTOM
CAMOUFLAGING	ENDLESS	REVERSIBLE
	IMPOSSIBLE	UNSTABLE

See the answer on page 378.

Find the words in the puzzle list within the matrix of letters. Words can be found oriented up, down, perpendicular, or reversed. When the puzzle is complete, unused letters at the top of the puzzle will spell out a related phrase reading left to right, and down.

```
O R T H O G R A P H I C P R O J E C T I O N I M
P O S L L A F R E T A W S S E L D N E S I B I L
L A E R M O R F T S I W T F L A H E N O I E T R
Y L I N I T S P U R E S T F O R E M . B T L N E
K Y A Z N X X M B K J C B N C S Q N P W T G K H
H E F N J F L R K F Y N O M O L E O C X E N M C
Y T T L O N C W K H P G Y R X N D I N B R A O S
T I C E G I H H B F A K N Z D R J T J W A I B E
I N M N R B S K R X N E M L J D B A X L U R I S
L L M P T P T N E H P Q E L M R H M X I Q T U I
I T L L O F L H E R C S R Q M A K R V M S E S L
B R N N D S W E E M S R K C J V K O M P E L B E
I N H Y J O S G D S I B L O J S Z F N O L B A N
S N G T L E O I T O F D S T Z R W S J S B I N R
S N K L P R R A B R R H O D K E H N T S I S D O
O B O N H Z I R L L S D Z W L T R A R I S S M C
P H V N H R G M Y U E N N Y T U P R L B S O V S
M M V R C Z W M M A P O K A L E Y T N L O P Q I
I R X A R H Q M N M N D B V S R L S L E P M Y T
R Z S G J T E K T W P D G J Z R N E L C M I T I
X E K W L R Y K D T N R R M E A H M J R I L X R
M V M C S R M B L K N Q X U C C J A X A P M N U
N T R I B A R D E S I G N R S S T N N T K M V A
H C N C Q Z J L P M M Z K M Z O K K C E D K K M
```

Ames Transformation	Josh Summers
Endless Staircase	Mauritis Cornelis Escher
Endless Waterfall	Mobius Band
Hollow Hexagon	One Half Twist from Real
Impossibility	Orthographic Projection
Impossible Crate	Oscar Reutersvard
Impossible Object	Roger Penrose
Impossible Square	Sandro del Prete
Impossible Triangle	Tribar Design
Jerry Andrus	Two Dimensional

See the answer on page 378.

Even as a maze, the Lincoln's hat illusion works! The hat is exactly as tall as its brim is wide. Get a ruler!

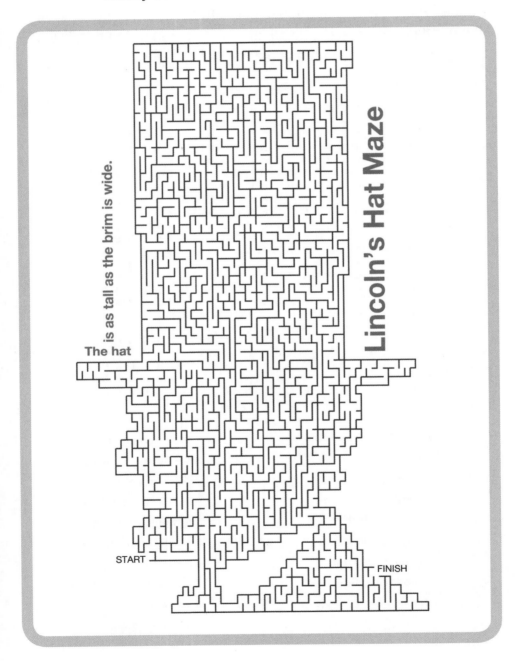

The hat is as tall as the brim is wide.

Lincoln's Hat Maze

START

FINISH

See the answer on page 379.

Become an illusion artist and draw your own optical illusion.
Follow the directions to complete this puzzle.

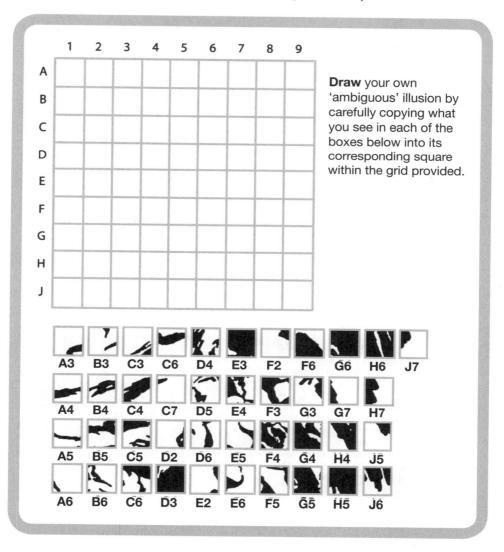

Draw your own 'ambiguous' illusion by carefully copying what you see in each of the boxes below into its corresponding square within the grid provided.

See the answer on page 379.

skill—usion 2

Become an illusion artist and draw your own optical illusion.
Follow the directions to complete this puzzle.

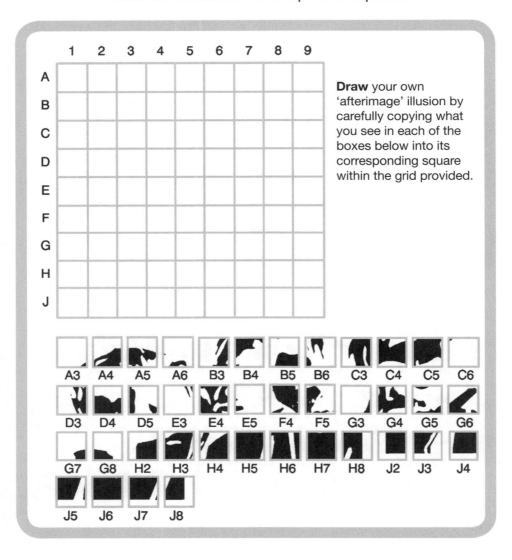

Draw your own 'afterimage' illusion by carefully copying what you see in each of the boxes below into its corresponding square within the grid provided.

See the answer on page 380.

Become an illusion artist and draw your own optical illusion. Follow the directions to complete this puzzle.

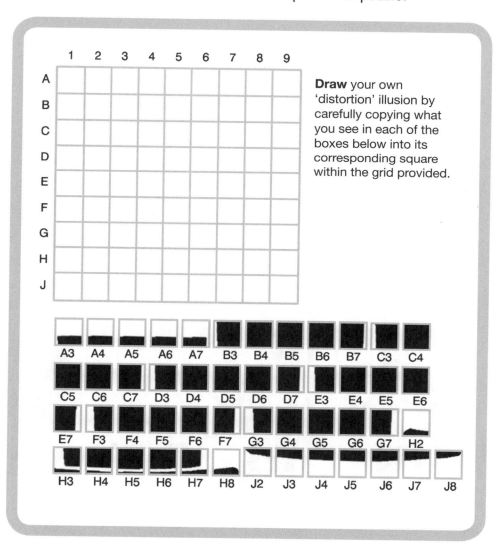

Draw your own 'distortion' illusion by carefully copying what you see in each of the boxes below into its corresponding square within the grid provided.

See the answer on page 380.

Become an illusion artist and draw your own optical illusion.
Follow the directions to complete this puzzle.

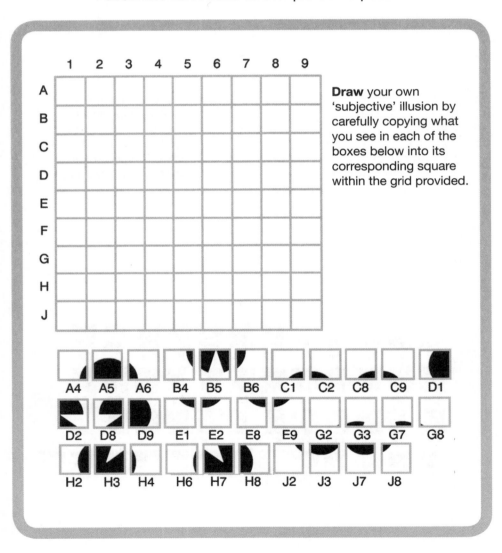

Draw your own 'subjective' illusion by carefully copying what you see in each of the boxes below into its corresponding square within the grid provided.

See the answer on page 381.

Become an illusion artist and draw your own optical illusion.
Follow the directions to complete this puzzle.

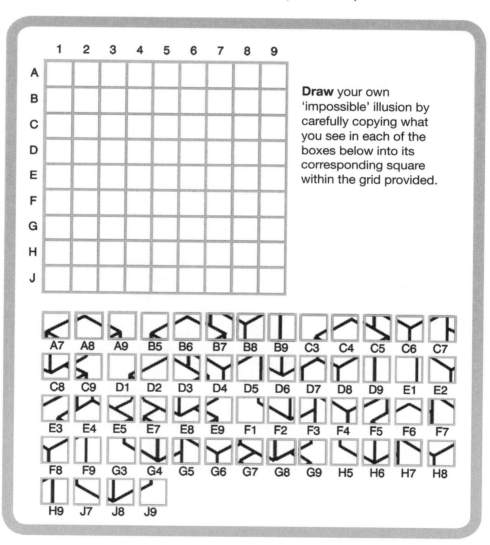

Draw your own 'impossible' illusion by carefully copying what you see in each of the boxes below into its corresponding square within the grid provided.

See the answer on page 381.

367

This maze takes its shape from Titchener's Illusion.
Which of the black circles looks bigger? They are both the same size.
Have fun with the maze.

See the answer on page 382.

Find the words in the puzzle list within the matrix of letters. Words can be found oriented up, down, perpendicular, or reversed. When the puzzle is complete, unused letters at the top of the puzzle will spell out a related phrase reading from left to right and down.

```
V I S U A L C O R T E X O H U M B A C
W D N V I S I O N I S P A N I L S N O
E N O R T E L S L E T C T Q A E L C L
I U P Y E W K R T I T R N C N T X Q O
V O T M H T G K C E A B K O D M M Y R
F R I N P G I D D L A A C T T G Q Y V
O G C T N T I N U N N D Y M T Q R C I
D E N K Y S D C A D N R Y B G N H L S
L R E G C M O R W A D Q O C J B K L I
E U R K H N C H S Y L T M T A K X A O
I G V M I T I D D L X P R B P M N B N
F I E B S T O P S D N I L B Y E T E Z
J F M G E R M Z C J Z G G Y C X C Y T
L A C I M E H C O T O H P K W F B E F
Q R G Z M H I G H C O N T R A S T L R
Y X H K T R A N S P A R E N C Y W J R
C W Q T N O I S U L L I L A C I T P O
S T E R E O S C O P I C V I S I O N L
K V L L O C C L U S I O N Q T K G R D
```

Binocular	Optic Nerve
Black and White	Photochemical
Blind Spots	Receptor
Eyeball	Retina
Field of View	Rods and Cones
Figure Ground	Steady Cam
High Contrast	Stereoscopic Vision
Occlusion	Transparency
Optical Illusion	Visual Cortex
Optic Disc	

See the answer on page 382.

This Yin-Yang Mouse Maze is the ultimate symbol of what the universe stands for, right–wrong, black–white, good–evil, or cheese–pepperoni. If you also see a mouse, you are well on the path to happiness.

START

FINISH

See the answer on page 383.

Here is a maze in the Ying-Yang Tao symbol. Have fun!

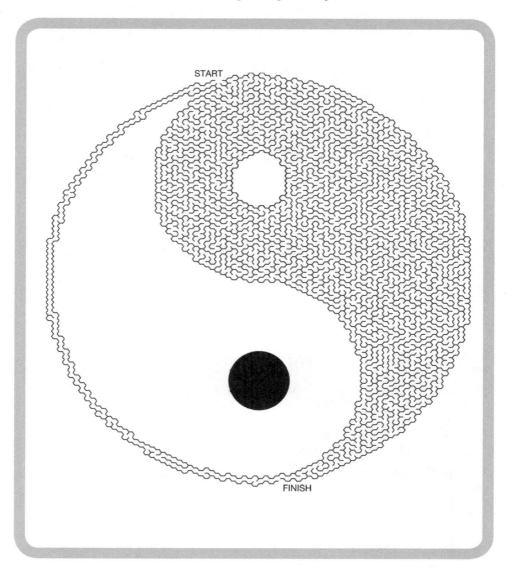

See the answer on page 383.

371

solutions—chapter 6

Page 235

solutions—chapter 8

Page 293

Page 295

Page 296

Page 301

solutions—chapter 9

Page 306

Page 318

Page 319

Page 322

Page 323

Page 346

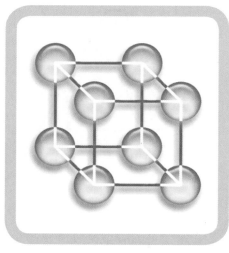

Page 347

solutions—chapter 11

Page 351

solutions—chapter 12

Page 352

Page 354

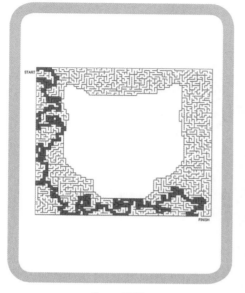

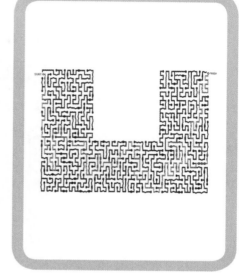

Page 357

Page 358

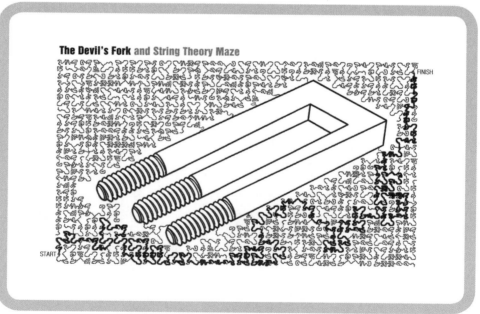

The Devil's Fork and String Theory Maze

Page 359

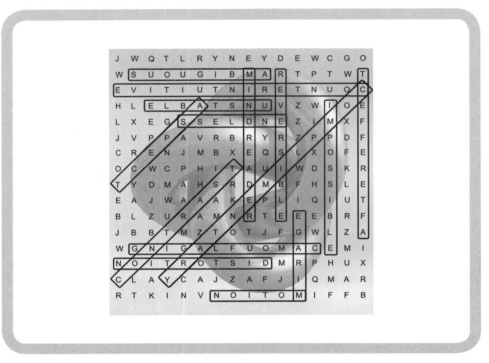

Page 360

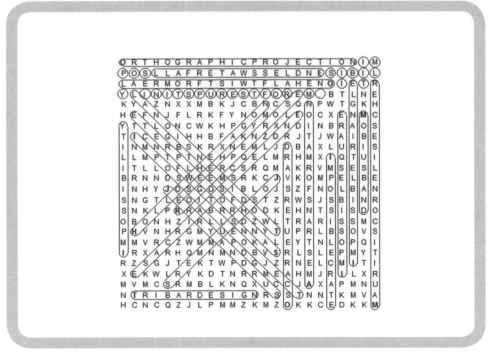

Page 361

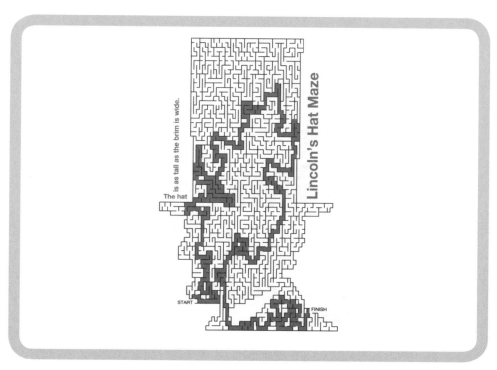

Page 362

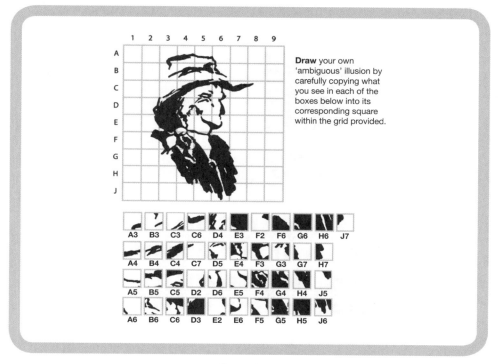

Draw your own 'ambiguous' illusion by carefully copying what you see in each of the boxes below into its corresponding square within the grid provided.

Page 363

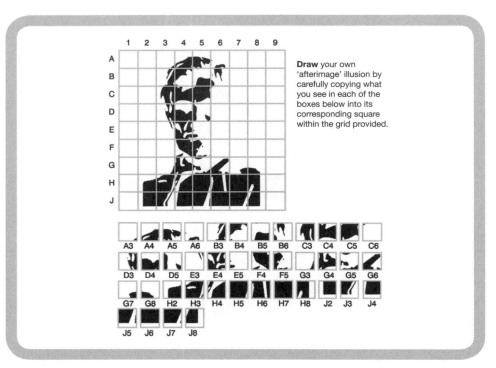

Draw your own 'afterimage' illusion by carefully copying what you see in each of the boxes below into its corresponding square within the grid provided.

Page 364

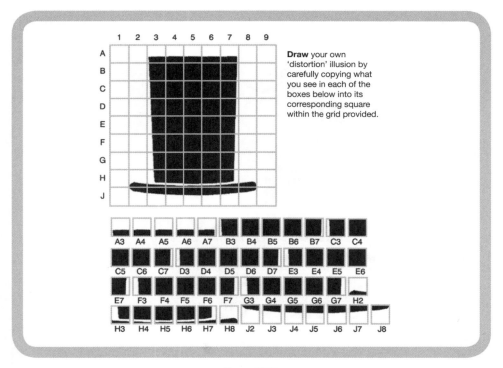

Draw your own 'distortion' illusion by carefully copying what you see in each of the boxes below into its corresponding square within the grid provided.

Page 365

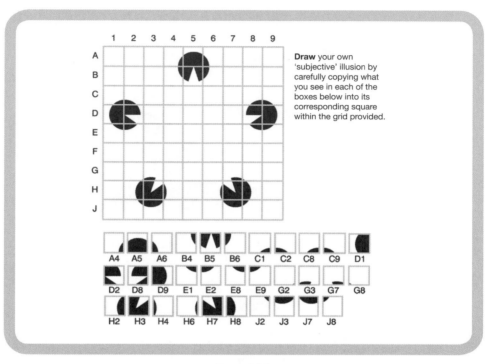

Page 366

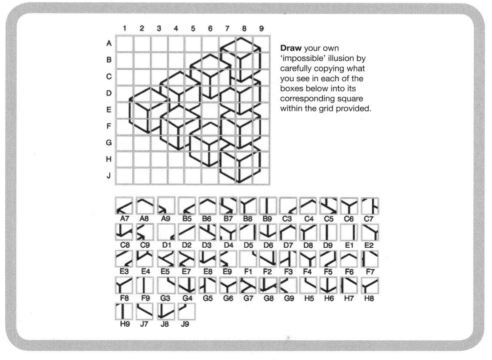

Page 367

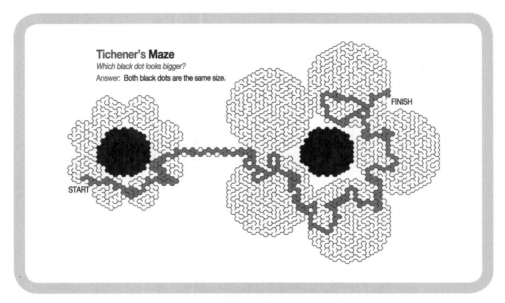

Tichener's Maze
Which black dot looks bigger?
Answer: Both black dots are the same size.

Page 368

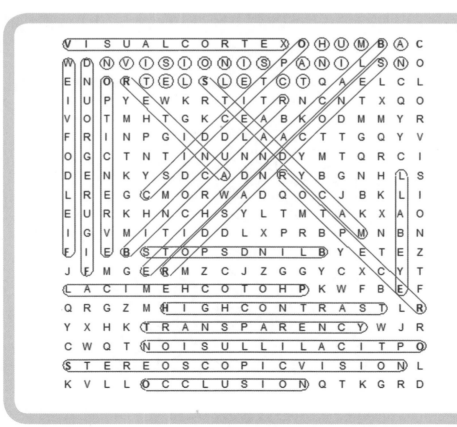

Page 369

Page 370

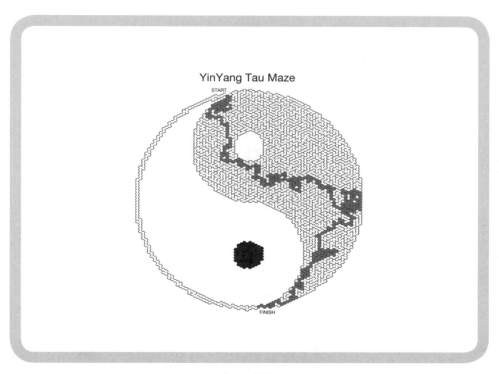

Page 371

photo credits

R. Ausbourne – SandlotScience.com: 24, 107, 110, 111, 122, 123, 138, 197, 206, 215, 223, 243, 250, 254, 255, 256, 257, 258, 260, 261, 262, 263, 264, 267, 269, 273, 274, 275, 277, 348, 349, 351

© R. Ausbourne – SandlotScience.com: 64, 72, 87, 99, 177, 178, 179, 180, 181, 182, 288, 290, 293, 314, 315, 317, 319, 321, 324, 328, 330, 332, 326, 334, 342, 343, 344, 345, 346, 347, 352, 354, 355, 356, 357, 358, 359, 360, 361, 362, 363, 364, 365, 366, 367, 368, 369, 370, 371, 376, 377, 378, 379, 380, 381, 382, 383

© 2006 Adamantios: 144

Paul Agule: 113

© 2006 Airair: 148

Giuseppe Arcimboldo: 162

© Arthur Azevedo: 59, 76, 222, 232, 233

© Arthur Azevedo – SandlotScience.com: 336, 337, 338, 339

© 2007 Paddy Breahnach Films: 116

© 2007 C.H. Brittenham: 140

© 2008 BrokenSphere: 156

L. Evens: 318, 319

Charles Allen Gilbert: 54

© 2008 Greg Hemmings: 150

William Hogarth: 130, 268

W. E. Hill: 135

Hans Holbein the Younger: 306

Wenzel Hollar: 134

© Prof. Bernd Lingelbach & Dr. Michael Schrauf: 196, 228, 249

R. Beau Lotto: 237

Gabriel Max: 96

Peter Newell: 173, 174, 175, 184, 185, 186

Northrop/Grummand: 137

L. Prang & Co.: 125

© 2008 Julius Reque: 142

© 1968 Rijksmuseum van Natuurlijke Historie, Leiden, Netherlands: 149

William Heath Robinson: 136

HM Rose: 94

© 2008 C. Dale Stillman: 143

© 2008 Bowie Snowgrass: 159

John Tenniel: 61

Gustav Verbeek: 188, 189, 190, 191

© 1998 Jeff Williams, 84

Rex Whistler: 192, 193

George Wotherspoon: 90, 124